FAQs for TAs

The ways in which schools are staffed, and the deployment of those staff members, are changing. Along with workforce remodelling and a new professionalism in schools has come a range of support roles designed to enable teachers to deliver as effective an education as possible. Teaching assistants (TAs) are key in this development and with their growing responsibilities and a clear career path come inevitable questions about how best to deliver that support to teachers and create the most efficient and effective working relationships. *FAQs for TAs* takes genuine questions and concerns of both new and established TAs and offers practical advice and solutions. From the very first chapter, which explores the role of the TA in schools and what the job entails, right through to the last, which looks at all the latest hot education topics that TAs need to be familiar with, this book has every base covered.

Organised into logical sections, the book covers issues such as:

- finding and applying for jobs
- how to be successful at interview
- plotting a career path
- relationship building with pupils, parents and colleagues
- managing and supporting pupils' behaviour.

Presented in question and answer format and carefully designed so that it can either be read from cover to cover or dipped into as appropriate, TAs will find its friendly, down-to-earth approach both supportive and informative. Being so strongly based in the reality of day-to-day life for TAs in primary and secondary schools gives the book true relevance, enabling readers to discover all they need to know to gain as much satisfaction in their work with teachers and pupils as possible.

Elizabeth Holmes is a professional writer specialising in education. Among her many published works is the highly respected book *FAQs for NQTs*. She also writes a weekly e-newsletter called *CPD Week*. In addition, Elizabeth is a freelance educational consultant contributing to the work of a number of specialist bodies including the Teacher Support Network and Optimus Professional Learning. You can also find out more about her work at www.elizabethholmes.co.uk

FAQs for TAs

Practical advice and working
solutions for teaching assistants

Elizabeth Holmes

Routledge
Taylor & Francis Group

LONDON AND NEW YORK

First published 2007 by Routledge
2 Park Square, Milton Park, Abingdon, Oxon OX14 4RN

Simultaneously published in the USA and Canada
by Routledge
270 Madison Ave, New York, NY 10016

*Routledge is an imprint of the Taylor & Francis Group,
an informa business*

© 2007 Elizabeth Holmes

Typeset in Garamond and Gill by BC Typesetting Ltd, Bristol
Printed and bound in Great Britain by
MPG Books Ltd, Bodmin

British Library Cataloguing in Publication Data
A catalogue record for this book is available from the British Library

Library of Congress Cataloging in Publication Data
Holmes, Elizabeth, 1969–
    FAQs for TAs: practical advice and working solutions for
    teaching assistants/Elizabeth Holmes.
       p.   cm.
    ISBN-13: 978–0–415–41105–9 (paperback)
    1. Teachers assistants – Handbooks, manuals, etc. I. Title.
    LB2844.1.A8H55   2007
    371.14'124–dc22
    2006030143

ISBN10: 0–415–41105–X (pbk)
ISBN10: 0–203–96364–4 (ebk)

ISBN13: 978–0–415–41105–9 (pbk)
ISBN13: 978–0–203–96364–7 (ebk)

Contents

Introduction

Deciding to become a teaching assistant (TA) is an incredibly exciting step to take. The role of TAs in schools is expanding significantly
right now along with the numbers of TAs themselves. The latest
government figures available (January 2006) show that there are
152,800 support staff in state-maintained schools in England, with
approximately three times more in primary schools than in secondary
schools. That's a very substantial number and all the evidence
suggests this will continue to rise in coming years.

As well as joining an ever-expanding team of support staff in our
schools, you are also hitting the world of education at a time of
developing professionalism. Workforce remodelling and other significant initiatives in education are leading to transformations in the
way in which pupils and teachers are supported in the classroom,
and TAs are right at the very heart of these changes.

If the last time you were in a school was as a pupil, you probably
wouldn't recognise TAs as we know them today. They are not merely
teachers' helpers, mixing paint and creating displays (although they
were important functions in their day!). The TAs of today are genuine
teaching assistants, often forming a bridge between pupils and
teachers, with far-reaching roles and responsibilities and the potential
to lead schools should they so desire! As a TA, you will not simply be

an extra pair of hands, you will play a central role in raising pupil attainment, and you will be unique and valuable for what you achieve for schools and pupils' learning.

This book evolved from the growing number of TAs posing questions in the popular staffroom forums on the internet. Its purpose is not to teach you how to do your job, there are other sources for that kind of information, not least the professionals who you will be working with. Rather, its purpose is to give new and would-be (and also experienced) TAs the answers to those niggling questions that can stand in the way of working with efficiency and excellence.

Many of the questions and answers covered in this book are equally applicable to TAs working in both the primary and secondary phases and, although it is England-specific, it is relevant in the other countries of the UK too. Overseas teachers and TAs may also find it of value in gaining a perspective on the system of TAs in schools in the UK.

If you take just one clear message from this book it should be this: there is always a source of advice and support if you need it. You *never* have to struggle on alone if you are experiencing difficulties or if you need support to improve your effectiveness at school. It's also important to remember the immense amount of enjoyment that can be had from a career in a school. Yes, it's busy and demanding, but there is very little to compare with the satisfaction of working closely with colleagues to ensure that the young people you support become the best they can be. As a TA, you are a crucial part of that – take time to acknowledge it!

Any book such as this cannot hope to cover *every* issue facing TAs, or *every* question that a TA may have. But combined with the support and advice available in your school and from your local authority, you should have all bases covered. While I hope that I have at least touched on all of the most important aspects of the role, if you feel that a particular question should be included, you can email me at eh@elizabethholmes.co.uk.

Latest information

The teaching profession is a dynamic one and changes occur quite often. Although the information in this book is correct at the time of going to press, the further information boxes contain information, websites and contacts from where the latest updates can be sourced.

Author's note

The advice in this book is for information and guidance only and is not intended to replace that of qualified practitioners. Neither the author nor the publisher can be held responsible for any consequences that occur as a result of following the guidance contained herein.

Acknowledgements

I would like to say a heartfelt thank you to the wonderful team of TAs at Thomas A'Becket First School in West Sussex, and in particular to Karen Free. Your advice and feedback was immensely helpful in putting this book together. In addition, Maggie Brackley, head-teacher at Thomas A'Becket First School, offered incredibly useful insights into the TA's role in schools, not to mention advice on actually getting a job as a TA.

I would also like to thank those teachers and TAs who have contacted me via my website (www.elizabethholmes.co.uk) and via the staffroom forum at www.eteach.com asking and answering many questions linked to the work of TAs. I continue to learn much from you all.

Finally I would like to thank Philip Mudd and the Routledge team, and Charlotte Howard of Fox and Howard Literary Agency for your support, encouragement . . . and patience!

CHAPTER I

The role of the TA

To define is to destroy, to suggest is to create.

(Stéphane Mallarmé)

Introduction

If you are considering becoming a TA, or have already taken the plunge, it's important to appreciate that although there are key types of activities that TAs are typically involved in for their work in schools, there is no set list of tasks that all TAs must do. The role is a broad one and schools deploy TAs in the way that works best for them (within reason). In addition, once TAs get into the swing of the job and start bringing to it their own unique skills and abilities, they build a role for themselves in the school that serves to support the pupils, teachers and the curriculum, which is tailor-made for the context in which they work.

For this reason, it is impossible to identify precisely what it is that effective TAs do and what, exactly, the role entails, although there are many common features of TAs' work in schools, not least the task of making learning *attractive*. This chapter seeks to offer some clarity on how you might expect to spend your working time as a TA, as well as offering some background to the role.

FAQs in this chapter cover:

- National standards for TAs
- Types of TA
- Minimum qualifications to become a TA
- National Workload Agreement
- Qualifications for TAs
- The structure of the NVQ/SVQ Level 2 for Teaching Assistants
- The structure of the NVQ/SVQ Level 3 for Teaching Assistants
- Other qualifications for TAs
- What TAs actually do
- The main features of the role of TAs
- Characteristics of effective TAs
- Good practice

Are there any national standards for TAs?

Yes there are. The National Occupational Standards for Teaching/
Classroom Assistants were originally developed by the Local Government National Training Organisation (in consultation with school
support staff, school managers and local authority officers across
the UK). They were designed to be suitable for use in schools
throughout the countries of the UK and represent 'best practice
expectations about the role and responsibilities of teaching/classroom
assistants' (Teaching Classroom Assistants Standards, April 2001).
The standards can be used in a variety of ways, not least as a basis
for the National and Scottish Vocational Qualifications (NVQs/
SVQs).

There are a number of values and principles underpinning the
National Occupational Standards, as follows:

- *Working in partnership with the teacher* — it is the teacher who sets
  the framework in which TAs work, and what TAs do in the classroom is under the direction of the teacher. The working relationship between teacher and TA needs to be close and effective.

- *Working within statutory and organisational frameworks* – TAs are responsible for working to agreed school policies and procedures and also need to be aware of wider statutory frameworks that impact on their work with pupils.
- *Supporting inclusion* – TAs should support the setting of suitable learning challenges that respond to the needs of pupils.
- *Equality of opportunity* – TAs have a role in ensuring that pupils have equal access to learning and development opportunities. This means working with individuals, small groups or whole classes depending on the direction from the teacher.
- *Anti-discrimination* – TAs must follow school regulations and policies relating to discrimination and must not discriminate against any individual or group on the grounds of gender, race, religion, cultural or social background, disability or sexual orientation.
- *Celebrating diversity* – TAs should value pupils' personal characteristics to develop their self-esteem and sense of identity.
- *Promoting independence* – TAs have a role in encouraging independence, self-reliance, learning skills, self-responsibility and increased subject knowledge in the pupils they work with.
- *Confidentiality* – TAs must adhere to school policies on confidentiality.
- *Continuing professional development* (*CPD*) – TAs should take advantage of planned and incidental development opportunities so that they can improve the contribution they make to raising pupil achievement.

The Training and Development Agency for Schools (TDA) is responsible for reviewing the National Occupations Standards for Teaching/Classroom Assistants. At the time of writing, such a review is currently being undertaken, as well as a review of the structure of NVQs based on the new standards. A fully updated set of Standards will be posted on the TDA website when they have been published. The National Occupations Standards for Teaching/Classroom Assistants are separate from the Standards for Higher Level Teaching Assistants (see Chapter 9).

I've heard TAs described as all sorts of things.
Are there significant differences between the terms
that schools use for different support staff?

It does get confusing but for the sake of clarity it's useful to consider the definitions set out by the TDA as follows:

Teaching assistants (TAs)

TAs work alongside teachers in the classroom, helping pupils with their learning on an individual or group basis. Some specialise in areas such as literacy, numeracy, special educational needs (SEN), music, English as an additional language (EAL) and the creative arts.

Higher level teaching assistants (HLTAs)

HLTAs are experienced TAs who plan and deliver learning activities under the direction of a teacher and assess, record and report on pupils' progress. They may also manage other classroom-based staff or may supervise a class in a teacher's absence. To find out more about this role see the HLTA section (in Chapter 9).

Nursery nurses

Nursery nurses work in cooperation with a teacher, looking after the social and educational development of children. Their work involves planning and supervising activities and keeping parents up to date with their child's progress.

Cover supervisors

Cover supervisors are suitably trained school staff who supervise pupils when teaching staff are absent.

For further information about the TDA's definition of the roles of various school support staff, take a look at the TDA website: www.tda.gov.uk/support/learningsupportstaff.aspx. You can also find out more about the various support roles in schools by logging on to www.skills4schools.org.uk.

What are the minimum qualifications required to become a TA?

The short answer is that there aren't any nationally set minimum qualifications. It is possible to become a TA with no qualifications at all.

What impact did the National Workload Agreement have on the role of TAs in schools?

The Agreement, known as *Raising Standards and Tackling Workload: A National Agreement*, meant the introduction of a number of important changes to teachers' conditions of service. These have been phased in over several years to address teacher workload issues. A central aspect of this Agreement has been the reform of support staff roles that now play an even more important part in reducing teachers' workloads.

In answer to the question, the impact on TAs has been great. There is now the widespread recognition in schools that teachers are not always the most appropriate people to perform certain tasks and that those supporting the core teaching and learning outcomes of the school have key roles to play. In order to move through this transitional period of change, schools have organised school change teams of which TAs have been members. This has helped to ensure that TAs' voices have been heard throughout the school remodelling process.

In short, the role of TAs has expanded in response to the Agreement and can now be viewed not only as a clear and distinct role in itself but also as part of a collection of support roles that lead right up to HLTAs and possibly beyond to qualified teacher status (QTS). The Agreement has helped to develop a new professionalism among TAs and with this has come enhanced responsibilities and arguably, a more central position in schools.

You can find out more about *Raising Standards and Tackling Workload: A National Agreement* from the TDA website: www.tda. gov.uk/remodelling/nationalagreement.aspx.

Is it possible to get a job as a TA without having any connections with the school already?

Yes it is. You don't need to have any prior connections with a school in order to work there as a TA. As long as you satisfy the school's selection criteria and they consider you to be the best person for the job, you can work there. That said, people who are thinking about becoming a TA often volunteer in schools first in order to get hands-on experience of what the role entails and then, when they have this insight, they can start to pursue jobs usually with a greater chance of success. This is quite often in a school that the would-be TA already has an involvement in, perhaps as a parent, but it doesn't have to be.

TAs form part of a distinct group of support staff in schools. They are not parent helpers, but rather are employed by schools to perform specific tasks in order to support the work of teachers and the achievement of pupils.

Are there any qualifications that I can obtain to help me to become a TA?

Yes there are. As there is no national minimum standard for qualifications for TAs, you will need to contact your local college of further education to find out what courses they run for TAs and what qualifications you can go for. These qualifications are commonly NVQs (SVQs in Scotland) at Levels 2 and 3.

NVQs for TAs tend to be modular and those taking them choose a blend of modules to suit what they are doing as a TA in school. There are some core modules that everyone takes and then some optional modules that can be chosen according to experience, interest and need.

NVQs are work-related, competence-based qualifications. Basically, they are designed to reflect the skills and knowledge that are needed in order to do a particular job effectively. NVQs are based on National Occupational Standards, which set out what competent people in that profession should be able to do. NVQs do not have to be completed within a specific period of time (within reason) and there are no entry requirements or age restrictions.

NVQs are organised into five levels. The NVQs designed for TAs are typically at Levels 2 and 3. The descriptions for those levels are as follows:

- Level 2: Competence that involves the application of knowledge in a significant range of varied work activities, performed in a variety of contexts. Some of these activities are complex or non-routine and there is some individual responsibility or autonomy. Collaboration with others, perhaps through membership of a work group or team, is often a requirement.
- Level 3: Competence that involves the application of knowledge in a broad range of varied work activities performed in a wide variety of contexts, most of which are complex and non-routine. There is considerable responsibility and autonomy and control or guidance of others is often required.

For further information on NVQs, check out the Qualifications and Curriculum Authority (QCA) website: www.qca.org.uk/14-19/qualifications/index_nvqs.htm.

What is the structure of the NVQ/SVQ Level 2 for Teaching Assistants?

Basically there are seven units of competence from the National Occupational Standards to be achieved. Four of these are mandatory and three are optional, for you to select depending on the requirements of your job and your career aspirations. These optional units would usually be decided in consultation with your school's head.

The mandatory units that all candidates must achieve are:

- help with classroom resources and records
- help with the care and support of pupils
- provide support for learning activities
- provide effective support for your colleagues.

The optional units that candidates can choose from (three must be selected) are:

- support literacy and numeracy activities in the classroom
- contribute to the management of pupil behaviour
- support the maintenance of pupil safety and security
- contribute to the health and well-being of pupils
- support the use of information and communications technology (ICT) in the classroom.

> You can find out more about the NVQ/SVQ Level 2 for Teaching Assistants from the TDA website: www.tda.gov.uk.

What is the structure of the NVQ/SVQ Level 3 for Teaching Assistants?

In order to complete the NVQ/SVQ to Level 3, candidates must achieve ten units of competence from the National Occupational Standards. There are four mandatory units and six optional units.

The mandatory units that all candidates must achieve are:

- contribute to the management of pupil behaviour
- establish and maintain relationships with individual pupils and groups
- support pupils during learning activities
- review and develop your own professional practice.

The optional units that candidates can choose from (six must be selected and the selection must include one unit from each of the sets A, B, C and D plus two more) are:

Set A

- assist in preparing and maintaining the learning environment
- contribute to maintaining pupil records
- observe and report on pupil performance
- contribute to the planning and evaluation of learning activities.

Set B

- promote pupils' social and emotional development
- support the maintenance of pupil safety and security
- contribute to the health and well-being of pupils
- provide support for bilingual/multilingual pupils
- support pupils with communication and interaction difficulties
- support pupils with cognition and learning difficulties
- support pupils with behavioural, emotional and social development needs
- provide support for pupils with sensory and/or physical impairment.

Set C

- support the use of ICT in the classroom
- help pupils to develop their literacy skills

- help pupils to develop their numeracy skills
- help pupils to access the curriculum.

Set D

- support the development and effectiveness of work teams
- develop and maintain working relationships with other professionals
- liaise effectively with parents.

> You can find out more about the NVQ/SVQ Level 3 for Teaching Assistants from the TDA website: www.tda.gov.uk.

Are there any other qualifications available for would-be TAs to do?

Yes there are. You would need to get in touch with your local further education and higher education colleges to find out more about what's available in your area, but the types of courses available are typically foundations degrees, skills for life qualifications in literacy and numeracy and introductory training programmes for support staff in schools.

> You can also find out more about the types of courses available for TAs in your area from your local authority. You'll find the contact telephone number in your Yellow Pages.

What is it that TAs actually do?

This isn't an easy question to answer as the role is broad and varied and headteachers and class teachers deploy their TAs in a variety of ways (see below for further details). One thing to keep in mind, though, is that both words in the job role title are active. The word 'teaching' is important as TAs do indeed teach pupils, although largely not to whole classes at a time, and the word 'assistant' reflects the core of the role. It is important to acknowledge the fact that TAs are *teaching* assistants and not just *teachers'* assistants. TAs who are well deployed in the classroom make an incredibly valuable contribution to teaching *and* learning and can have a significant impact on the attainment achieved by pupils.

In essence, TAs provide support for teachers, pupils, the school as a whole and the curriculum taught within the school. But it is a broad role with many interpretations within that framework.

What are the main features of the role of a TA?

Again, this is a difficult question to answer, in fact it is an impossible question to answer, as the role will vary depending on the school. However, all TAs will be involved to a greater or lesser extent in the following:

- helping the pupils they work with to become independent learners (as independent as possible)
- helping pupils to participate in the opportunities available to them at the school
- helping to raise the standards achieved by pupils
- supporting the delivery of the national strategies for literacy and numeracy
- helping to develop classroom materials for pupils
- helping to ensure that pupils stay on task as much as possible
- working with pupils to develop their social skills
- working with the teacher and pupils to ensure that the school's behaviour policy is adhered to
- helping pupils with physical needs
- detecting any bullying that may be occurring and intervening as appropriate
- making sure that all children are included in the experiences the school has to offer

- enabling the teacher to work with small groups
- helping teachers to implement their lesson plans
- liaising with outside agencies such as educational psychologists and speech therapists
- acting as a model of good practice for children to follow (for example in behaviour, spelling, language and so on)
- providing valuable feedback for teachers on the work and behaviour of pupils.

Above all else, the heart of the role of the TA is to provide support for the class teacher. It is from this that all other roles and responsibilities stem, and if the relationship between the TA and teacher is such that this support cannot be given fully, it is unlikely that the TA can support the pupils and the school effectively. The core relationship between the teacher and the TA is key to all the other features of the role of the TA.

What are the characteristics of an effective TA?

This is a tricky one to answer because naturally these characteristics vary according to the context in which the TA is working. In other words, a TA who is working really effectively in one school doing certain tasks and utilising particular skills may not be so effective in another school where the needs of the staff and pupils are significantly different.

That said, there are specific, general characteristics that all effective TAs tend to have and these are:

- a commitment to helping children to achieve their potential
- an ability to work effectively as part of a team
- a positive and willing nature
- flexibility and the ability to respond to changing needs, sometimes without notice.

If you have the above in abundance you will get on fine! If on the other hand you are slightly negative, inflexible, unwilling or unhappy to work as a team and so on, you will probably come up against continual problems at work as a TA and be unable to derive any sense of job satisfaction.

Working as a member of a team is particularly important for TAs. As a TA, you are not simply a member of the school's staff, you are part of a team – a crucial part. When thinking about the characteristics of effective TAs it is well worth taking the time to consider what you can bring to a team. If nothing else, this will be incredibly useful for the application and interview process when it comes to applying for a job. Ask yourself these questions:

- Would I be happy to work with a wide range of people from diverse backgrounds?
- Would I be good at offering my ideas for discussion?
- Would I follow through the tasks I am given as a result of team work?
- Would I suggest ways of making the most of new opportunities facing the team?
- Do I have the ability to sense what might need to be done without being told?
- Would I offer alternative suggestions freely and without an attachment to a particular outcome?
- Am I keen to get to know work colleagues and they way in which they operate in their jobs?
- Am I able to think beyond the obvious?
- Am I good at finding practical solutions to problems?
- Do I make good relationships with others?
- Can I remain purposeful when under pressure?
- Am I tactful yet honest?
- Am I happy to support the school's policies and put them into practice whenever necessary?
- Am I fully behind the ethos of the school?

Above all else, it's important to enjoy working with children if you are a TA. If you don't, they will sense this immediately!

How can a TA be expected to produce good practice without being told explicitly what to do?

This is a good point. It is essential for TAs to be given guidance, support and training in order to work to the highest standards possible within a school. Once you are fully immersed in the role you will find that you do not always need to be told precisely what to do as you will develop a way of working with the class teacher(s) that suits you both. You will be able to respond to the needs of the teacher and pupils with greater ease as your working relationship develops. If you find that you are more comfortable working to precise instructions, make sure that you communicate this to the teacher. It is important for you to understand how each other works most effectively and to find the middle ground between you that will lead to pupil progress.

> It is important to get into the habit of discussing with the teacher(s) you work with any issues regarding working practices sooner rather than later. Clear up any uncertainties as soon as they arise and you have a greater chance of keeping your working relationship as effective as possible.

CHAPTER 2

The job-hunting process

The first and most important step toward success is the feeling that we can succeed.

(Nelson Boswell)

Introduction

Deciding to pursue a career as a TA is only one step in the process. The next task is to find your ideal vacancy and bag your perfect job, or as close to perfect as you can make it. This isn't always as easy as it sounds, but with the right attitude and planning, it needn't become a nightmare either.

Knowing how and where to look for the ideal vacancy for you is the first step to take. You may need to employ a little patience too, but a positive mental attitude can help to ensure that you reach your goals with minimum disappointment.

Once you have found a job to go for, securing an interview and performing on the big day is the next challenge. This chapter looks at how you can best go about finding a job to apply for and how to improve your chances of getting through the selection process.

FAQs in this chapter cover:

- Finding vacancies for TA jobs
- Online job adverts
- Filling in the application form
- Referees
- What schools are looking for
- Making speculative applications
- Looking in the right places
- Interview nerves
- Interview questions
- TA characteristics
- What to wear
- Interview length
- Interviews in faith schools
- Changing your mind
- Temporary contracts

How do I find out where the vacancies for TAs are?

Most vacancies for TAs will be advertised on local authority websites (if you're not sure of the exact web address ring up the switchboard and they will be able to tell you – local authorities are usually county councils, borough councils or unitary authorities). Many local authorities also advertise such vacancies in local papers too so it's well worth scouring those for any possible opportunities. There may also be a local authority jobs bulletin that you could sign up for either in paper form or electronic form.

Are jobs ever advertised anywhere else?

Yes, the internet! Recruitment websites are huge in the world of education now so it is well worth making sure that you are looking at the right sites to track down your ideal vacancy. Staff 4 Schools specialises in recruiting support staff for schools. Find out more by visiting the website: www.staff4schools.com.

How do I go about applying for a job?

Once you have found a vacancy advertised that you would like to go for you will need to request an application form. The advert will tell you how to go about this. The form may be electronic if you are applying online or in paper form (still more usual) and you may have to get it from the local authority or from the school itself. If you are asked to send a stamped addressed envelope, be sure to ask specifically how much postage to put on the envelope. The last thing you want is for the form not to reach you because it's languishing in a pile of mail with insufficient postage in your local post office.

What do I need to know about filling in the application form?

First things first – take a photocopy of it. Or take two! You want to be able to do a dry run so the version you send in is as neat as possible. Don't under-estimate how important the presentation of your form is.

Next, read it through and gather together all the information you will need in order to answer it (personal details, education details, qualifications and relevant dates and so on).

There will be a section on the form asking you to write about your skills and competencies. The space for this is typically half a page but it can be more. In many ways, this is the most important part of the form. It is where you get an opportunity to show that you are exactly what the school is looking for. The best way of doing this is to take the following steps:

- Read the person specification (there is usually a written description of the personal qualities the school is looking for in applicants and this is most often called the 'person specification') as carefully as possible.

- Make a note of every skill and competence that you have that matches what the school is looking for. The aim is to address everything on the school's wish list.
- Aim to give examples of when and how you have used your relevant skills.
- Optimise the positive! What you write has to entice. Although it's important always to be honest, don't be negative at all.
- Make sure that what you write is perfect in spelling and grammar. If the form is handwritten, your handwriting needs to be clear and easy to read (if an adult can't make it out, the chances are a child won't be able to either – that's the kind of thought that goes through the minds of shortlisters!).
- Begin and end this section of the form with real impact.
- Include a sentence about what motivates you to be a TA.
- If you need more space than is provided on the form, it is acceptable to add a separate page if necessary. Don't take this as the go ahead to ramble though. Make sure what you write is concise and supportive of your application. Waffle, and readers will quickly tire.
- If possible, ask someone to read through your form before you write out the final version.
- Keep a photocopy of what you send in.
- Remember that this is where you are selling yourself. Don't be meek about it! It's a great opportunity to shine so make your application irresistible. You want the reader to be compelled to invite you for an interview. Once that's in the bag you're half way there!

If you are unsure about the quality of your application you may want to consider asking a local headteacher (preferably one you have a connection with) to look over it. Failing that, if you have any teacher or TA friends, or if you know a school governor, or just a trusted friend, it would be a good idea to ask them to read through your application to see if there is anything obvious you could improve on.

Who should I put down as a referee?

You may be asked for one or two referees and one should be your current (or recent) employer. Always ask the person's permission first before putting their details down on the form; you want them to be in a really good mood when they write your reference! If you don't have a relatively recent employer, perhaps because you have taken a career break, you will need to use someone who knows you in a professional capacity if at all possible. At the very least, your referee needs to be someone who can comment with authority on your suitability for the job.

What are schools looking for in the applications they receive?

There's no definitive checklist, but they are likely to be looking for the following:

- application forms that are filled in perfectly (no spelling or grammatical errors)
- the qualifications you have
- any previous connections you may have with the school
- the degree to which your skills and competencies match the person specification for the job.

I haven't seen a job advertised but there is a school that I would love to work at if a vacancy occurred. Is there anything that I can do about that?

Yes! It is always worth sending in a speculative application just in case it is held on record until a suitable vacancy is advertised. This may not be for a while, but at least you have expressed your interest in working at the school and most heads find this acceptable (if not slightly flattering!). The worst that can happen is that you receive a letter saying 'thank you but no thank you'.

When making a speculative application these ideas will help:

- Find out exactly who your letter should be addressed to (usually the headteacher).
- Keep your letter punchy and to the point, including your achievements, skills and competencies. The whole letter should be no more than one side of A4, and ideally shorter than that.
- Include a sentence to say that you are interested in a TA post at the school.
- Match your skills and experience to what you know of the school.
- Write something about what you feel you could bring to the school. Aim to give brief examples where possible.
- Ask for an interview and offer some possible dates. Don't be too specific – it's fine to say something along the lines of 'I can be available to visit your school over the next few weeks'.
- If you have a CV, include that too. Although this helps, it isn't vital.
- Use good quality paper for your letter and enclose a stamped addressed envelope.
- Make a follow-up phone call if you don't hear anything within a week or two.

You may not be successful immediately, but this approach can bring results and is worth trying if there is one particular school that you know you want to work at. It is also worth asking the head if you can volunteer at the school too. That way you get to find out more about the place and they get to see how great you'd be as an employee there!

Would I be able to go for a job in the same school that my children attend?

Yes, there is nothing to stop you from doing this if you want to. There are plenty of teachers and TAs who work in the same school their children attend and this can work fine. You may prefer not to work in the same class as your child but most schools can accommodate this.

I haven't seen any jobs advertised at all. What do I do?

It could be that there are not abundant jobs for TAs in your area at present, but equally, you may simply not be looking in the right places. Make sure that you are covering every base. Look in local papers, local authority websites, local jobs bulletins and on the internet. In addition, make sure people know about your intentions. Word of mouth is a great way of finding out about job vacancies.

Most local authorities will also have a recruitment strategy manager who focuses on vacancies in the teaching profession. It may be worth giving him/her a ring (ring the local authority switchboard to be put through) and asking about the local situation regarding schools' needs for TAs. You never know what their local knowledge might lead to!

Above all else, don't give up hope. You may not find your ideal job immediately, but it is always worth persisting when you know what you want. As long as you are looking in all the right places, you will find a vacancy to go for sooner or later, even if you have to widen your net a little or re-examine your ideals. Sometimes, additional flexibility can encourage us to consider possibilities we previously thought unworkable. Be as open as possible.

I get really nervous at the thought of interviews. What can I do to keep myself calm?

If you've been invited for an interview after going through the process of filling in and submitting your form, the last thing you want is for nerves to ruin your chances of being successful. The best way to manage nerves is to enjoy the interview! That may sound easier said than done, perhaps it is, but if you can enjoy the challenge of showing a headteacher that you are the most suitable person for the job and that you do truly want to work at that school, you'll have a far greater chance of walking out with the job.

There are many things that you can do to calm your nerves before an interview. If you feel that your nerves are getting completely out of hand you might want to talk to your GP. But there are other methods you can employ to keep nerves to a minimum that you might want to try first:

- Get plenty of sleep the night before an interview so that you're not nervous and stressed about it simply because you're tired. This can and does happen, yet a good night of refreshing sleep can transform the way you view an interview.
- Think carefully about what you eat the day before too, and on the morning of the interview. Plenty of fresh fruits and vegetables will help to ensure that you're clear-headed and ready for action.
- Be aware of how you are thinking about the interview. If you find yourself thinking negatively and in a self-defeatist way, turn those thoughts into positive ones. There is no reason why this job cannot be yours!
- Use deep, rhythmic breathing to calm feelings of panic.
- Consider using one of the harmless natural solutions to nervousness such as Bach Rescue Remedy or something similar. Many people swear by them. A good natural health store will help you to find something suitable for you.
- If nerves become a major issue and risk destroying your chances of even attending an interview, do consider addressing them specifically with a qualified practitioner. Homeopathy, reflexology, neuro-linguistic programming and aromatherapy are just some of the therapies available with a good track record in helping to calm nerves.

Remember, there is no need for excessive nerves at an interview. It's important to feel some sense of trepidation, as it's this that can propel you to perform to the best of your ability, but as soon as nerves start to hinder you it's time to do something about it.

> If your nerves really do seem to get out of control, make sure that you seek the advice of a qualified health care provider such as your GP.

What questions am I likely to be asked at an interview?

It is impossible to know what questions might come up and really, it's best if you don't know. It's usually pretty obvious for interviewers to spot when someone is reciting a scripted answer and that's not at all what they want to hear. What they want is spontaneous and inspired answers! However, there are some likely topics that may be covered. These ideas will help:

- Can you tell us why you have applied for the post? *They want to hear that you want to work at that school in particular, not in any school. Show that you know a bit about the place and are committed to being a part of its community.*
- What would you do if you disagreed with something the class teacher asked you to do? *They want to know that you would follow the instructions you were given. If you wanted to clarify why you were asked to do something, you would ask the teacher in private and not in front of any pupils.*
- What experience do you have of working with children in a pre-school setting? *Even if you have only worked as a volunteer this is worth talking about.*
- What experiences do you have of working with children/young people with SEN? *Aim to give examples that are as relevant to the job as possible. If you don't have any experience at all, it's fine to say that, although you might want to mention that you are familiar with certain conditions such as dyslexia, dyspraxia, attention deficit hyper-activity disorder (ADHD) and autistic spectrum disorders (ASDs).*
- We work as teams in this school. What qualities can you bring to a team? *Be honest! Mentioning things such as sense of humour, commitment, creativity and a hard-working attitude will always go down well.*

- What would you do if a child repeatedly wants to cuddle you? *Children get attached, but it's important to say that you would not cuddle the child, taking care not to reject, perhaps by holding its hand, and would discuss the situation with the class teacher. Excessive clinginess or inappropriate affection can be a sign of an underlying issue in the child's development or home life and this is just the sort of information that should be passed on to the teacher.*

- How would you deal with a child who refused to do as you asked? *They want to know what strategies you would employ and how long you would continue before seeking support and advice. This is just the sort of question where they are expecting you to go beyond the obvious. Many interview questions can be answered in a very similar way by all candidates but some, such as this one, can be 'decider' questions. Answer that you would use a range of strategies based on building on cooperation and initiative and firmly within the school's policy on behaviour, rewards and sanctions. You would also discuss the potential of such a problem arising with the teacher beforehand so that you have already arranged what you can do in such a situation.*

- What specific talents do you have? *Don't be shy! This is when they want to hear about any talents that might be of use to the school such as piano playing. Be honest, but don't hide behind modesty!*

- How would you handle a parent asking you direct questions about the school or one of its pupils? *This is a common question and is all about confidentiality. They want to know that you would not be discussing anything at all about what happens in the classroom with parents or others. There are appropriate channels that parents can use if they have any questions to ask and it is essential that as a TA, you respect the need for confidentiality.*

- What would you do if a child disclosed personal information to you about his/her life at home? *They want to know that you would pass this information onto the class teacher. This is essential. There may be child protection issues (CPIs) and the person in the school with responsibility for this may have to involve outside agencies. It's worth keeping in mind that as a TA you are likely to get pretty close to certain children and they may consider you to be trustworthy enough to start divulging a little of what may be going on for them at home.*

- How would you handle having to deal with a child who had soiled him or herself, or who had thrown up? *They need to know that you're not going to throw your hands up in horror and run from the classroom pinching your nose! If you will be working with young children, for example in the Foundation Stage, you may well come across one with continence issues and as a TA, there's a likelihood you'll be involved in any clean-up operations. Remember, you're part of a team! Saying that you'd get on with whatever needed doing is the right answer! You may like to ask the school about what arrangements it has in place to protect staff from accusations over CPIs. Although as an employee of the school you would have had a check done by the Criminal Records Bureau (CRB), some schools also ensure that tasks such as changing a child with continence problems are always done by two adults.*
- Do you have any questions to ask? *It's not essential to ask questions at this point. If you don't have any just say something along the lines of 'no thank you, all my questions have been covered'. If you have any questions about pay, ask them now. In particular make sure you understand the implications of being paid pro rata if that applies to the post. You should be given a rough idea of what the hourly rate for the job is.*
- If you were offered the post, would you accept it? *There's only really one answer once you get to this stage of proceedings. If you haven't withdrawn so far, your answer should be 'yes'. Remember, this does not constitute an offer of a job, but they do need to ascertain whether they should consider you when deliberating over who to offer the job to.*

You may also be asked questions designed to bring out your attitude to your involvement in the school as a community, SEN, equal opportunities in the classroom, CPD and so on. It would be worth considering what responses you might give.

If in doubt about how to deal with a scenario presented in an inter-view question, it's usually a safe bet to say that you would discuss it with the class teacher. Heads need to know that you would be com-mitted to working closely as a team with the class teacher and would ask about anything you were not sure about rather than making a potentially maverick decision. That's not passing the buck – it's fine to say you would want to talk it through. If the scenario is a tricky one, that's usually the response the head is looking for.

What characteristics does the ideal TA have?

The top of the list has to be being a team player. As a TA, you cannot be the type who needs autonomy. You will be given tasks to do and will have to work cohesively with the class teacher. At the same time, although you will be given instructions and be expected to follow them to the letter with respect for the teacher's authority, it is impor-tant that you are able to use your initiative. That sounds like an impossible demand, but there's a balance to be struck here and much will depend on the relationship you build with the teachers you work with.

As a TA, you are likely to find yourself working with a child with particular physical or learning needs. A willingness to read up on the conditions that children may be suffering from is important, as is a desire to learn on the job and adapt the way you work as necessary. Heads are also increasingly keen on employing TAs who are willing to go through the process to become an HLTA.

Whether you are working in the primary or secondary environ-ment, an awareness of the role of emotional intelligence in the class-room is essential. As a TA you will probably be working either one to one or with small groups, and relationships can become pretty intense. You may also be in a withdrawal situation, taking children outside the classroom, and having a background knowledge on how best to make those relationships work to maximise learning and emotional development is important.

What should I wear at an interview? Is it important?

It is important to show that you view interviews as being an opportunity to demonstrate your professionalism and your commitment to the job. Panels will want to see that you have made an effort and that you are treating the interview as different from a normal work day.

Aim to dress smartly and comfortably. Pay attention to the finer details of your outfit. Interviewers and interview panels have seen candidates with torn clothing, hems that are falling down, scuffed shoes, scruffy hair, garish make-up, buttons missing, dirty clothing – a full range of sartorial gaffes! All of these things are avoidable and do not cost much to correct. You don't need to turn up in a brand new outfit but one that is smart, clean and well cared for will get noticed and will reflect aspects of your character that are vital for taking pride in the job of TA. Keep accessories to a minimum too – less is always more – and aim to present an overall impression of neatness and calm!

> If you have any doubts about what you plan to wear to an interview test-drive your outfit by asking a trusted friend to give you some honest feedback. The aim is to be comfortable and at ease so that your confidence and suitability for the job can shine through.

How long is my interview likely to be?

Again, there are no hard and fast rules but typically an interview will be about 20 minutes to half an hour. You will also be given a tour of the school and may be given a chance to sit in on a class and observe what is happening.

I have an interview in a faith school. Will they ask me about my religious beliefs?

If you have an interview in a faith school (for example, a Catholic or Church of England school), the questions you are asked should be broadly similar to those you would be asked in a non-denominational school. However, you should expect to be asked something about your faith and how it would fit with the ethos and mission of the school. No one can predict what questions are asked in interviews, but it would be a good idea to think about how you might answer being questioned on the following:

• Do your beliefs complement those of the school? How can you demonstrate that? *They want to hear that you share the same faith and will actively support the school's ethos. Being part of the local church community will help. They may accept you not being actively involved in the particular religion but you would have to convince the head (and possibly governors) that you are able to support it despite this.*
• In what ways can you support the religious ethos of the school? *They will be looking for specifics here. Do you have examples from previous employment or voluntary work? Or perhaps from your involvement in a church?*

The head will need to be happy that you do not have any religious or philosophical objections to beliefs that underpin the work of the school. If you feel that this may be a problem for you, particularly after visiting the school and meeting the head, it's probably not a good idea to pursue your application. There will be other jobs more suitable.

> You may want to talk to your union about the employment implications of working in a faith school. At the very least you will need to establish exactly who your employer would be (usually the governing body of a faith school rather than the local authority).

What happens if I decide I don't want the job after attending an interview?

Although this is relatively unlikely, if you do decide that you don't want to work in a school once you have seen it in action, make sure you withdraw from the proceedings as early as possible. Be as sure as you can be though, because doing this will effectively prevent you from getting a job at the school in the future. That said, an interview is a two-way process. It's a time for you to assess the school as much as it is for the school to assess you. There's no point in continuing with the interview if you know beyond all doubt that the job at that school is not for you.

I have heard that TAs are sometimes appointed on a trial basis. If I am offered such an arrangement should I accept it?

This is entirely up to you but it is not uncommon for TAs to be appointed on a temporary contract for a specific reason. As long as any such arrangements are acceptable according to the school's and the local authority's employment policy, you can't really go wrong. Don't forget, such trial periods work two ways. While they can be an opportunity for the school to see how you work, they are also a chance for you to see how the school works and whether you could fit in with this on a long-term or permanent basis.

Any such trial period should have a clearly agreed end date by which the situation can be assessed and any needs for professional development can be discussed. Temporary contracts should never be indefinite.

Contact your union or local authority if you are at all unsure about the conditions of your employment. Don't let such concerns slide. It's always better to seek clarity sooner rather than later.

CHAPTER 3

Starting work as a TA

Find a job you like and you add five days to every week.
(H. Jackson Browne)

Introduction

You have managed to gain employment as a TA and are about to start work in a new school. But what should you expect? This is a near impossible question to answer as schools differ so much from one another that what goes in one might be unheard of in another. But there are key concerns that TAs typically have and these have been addressed below.

One thing to remember when starting your new job as a TA is that you will not be expected to 'know it all' right from the word go. Most schools are extremely understanding of the fact that it takes time to settle into new routines and ways of working. While you will be expected to be ready to launch into classroom work on the first day, you will not be expected to hit the ground running at the pace that an experienced TA in the school might be working at. It won't be until the second day until that's expected!

This chapter looks at what you might expect on starting work as a TA and how you can best settle into the job.

FAQs in this chapter cover:

- CRB checks
- Working without a CRB Disclosure
- Job descriptions
- Contracts
- Work mentors
- What to wear
- First aid
- Classroom organisation
- Joining a union
- Induction
- Using the staffroom
- Internal post
- Instructions for working
- Supporting all children
- Line managers
- Pupil records
- PEPs and IEPs
- Pupil personal care
- Year groups
- The National Curriculum

I have been told that I need to have a check done by the CRB. What does this entail?

According to its website the CRB exists 'to reduce the risk of abuse by ensuring that those who are unsuitable are not able to work with children and vulnerable adults'. It helps organisations in all sectors to identify candidates who should not be working with children.

The CRB checks police records and information held by the Department for Education and Skills (DfES) and the Department of Health to determine whether the applicant is suitable for employment (among other things). There are two levels of check: Standard and Enhanced:

- Standard Disclosures show current and spent convictions, cautions, reprimands and warnings held on the Police National Computer among others.
- Enhanced Disclosures contain the same information as the Standard Disclosure but with the addition of relevant information held by local police forces.

The checks are known as 'Disclosures' and as someone working in a school with children it is likely you will need the Enhanced Disclosure. On acceptance of a job, the school will usually arrange for a CRB check on you to be done. You will be told what the procedure is for this in your particular school.

> You can find out all you need to know about the CRB from its website: www.crb.gov.uk or by calling 0870 90 90 811. If you have any concerns at all about this process talk to your union or your local authority.

I know that my school has sent off for a CRB check for me but it hasn't arrived yet. Does that mean that I can't start work?

The DfES does allow those who have applied for a CRB check that hasn't yet been processed to start work in a school provided they are under supervision and they are not on List 99 (List 99 contains the names, dates of birth and teacher reference numbers of people whose employment has been barred or restricted, either on grounds of misconduct or on medical grounds).

That said, it would be up to your headteacher and governors to decide whether you can start work before a CRB check has been completed. If you are in any doubt about this, talk to your headteacher sooner rather than later.

You can find out more about List 99 from the DfES website: www.dfes.gov.uk.

Should I have received a job description before I start work?

In an ideal world, yes, you should. But this doesn't always happen until you actually start on your first day (sometimes it can take longer to get a written job description to you). That said, on your first day, you should be in no doubt about the broad scope of your job, which should have been made clear to you at the interview and when you accepted the position. If you do have doubts, aim to get clarification on these as soon as possible. Talk to the teacher(s) you are working with, or to your line manager or to the school's head-teacher.

As soon as you get your job description, read it through carefully and make sure that it fits your expectations of the job role. Your job description should clearly outline and define what it is that you are expected to do. If anything about it is ambiguous or open to interpretation it would be a good idea to discuss with your headteacher exactly what is expected of you and get the outcome of those discussions formalised in a revised job description. It may seem unnecessarily bureaucratic to go through this process, but it is worth it. You only need to do it once and it's always better to be crystal clear about these things than it is to be unsure or doubting; that's how resentment builds and in a school community there's no room for resentful staff. There is nothing that cannot be clarified, one way or another, through discussion.

What sort of contract can I expect as a newly employed TA?

This depends entirely on the school and its governors. Some TAs are given temporary contracts particularly if they have been employed to work with one specific child. This is because if, for whatever reason, the child leaves the school, the post is no longer needed. Some schools still employ TAs on permanent contracts in the knowledge that if one child with a particular need leaves the school the TA can usefully be deployed elsewhere in the school. This decision depends on the size of the school and the budgets available.

> If you have any questions or concerns about the contract you are given talk to your union. Never accept a contract that you either don't fully understand or you didn't expect. Your union will help you to sort out any contract issues that you may have.

What do I need to be aware of in my contract?

Everything! Make sure that you read and understand everything that it contains, particularly regarding the following:

- hours of work
- rates of pay and how this is distributed through an academic year
- holiday pay entitlements if applicable
- expectations regarding attendance at meetings and associated arrangements for pay
- whether time off in lieu is ever granted for occasions when non-classroom activities are undertaken at the request of the school
- expectations regarding the school's dress code (these are not commonly contained in the contract but can be).

As with any other aspect of your employment at a school, if there is anything that you are not certain about, ask for clarity. There is no limit to the number of questions you can ask! Try the class teacher first, then the headteacher and your union if you still have un-answered questions.

Will I be given a mentor when I start work as a TA?

There are no set rules about this but many schools do buddy new staff up with existing members of staff to help the settling-in process go more smoothly. This may be a fairly informal arrangement based on the practicalities of starting work in a new school, or it may be based on a more professional relationship geared towards improving performance.

Whatever the arrangements are at your school you should be told about them ideally before you start work. If you are not given a buddy or mentor and feel that you would appreciate one, talk to your head-teacher about the possibility of partnering up with someone suitable. It would be usual for existing TAs at the school to be involved in this kind of arrangement.

I haven't been told anything about what to wear when I start work. What should I do?

Some schools have a dress code that all staff are made aware of (or at least should be!) before they start work. Other schools have less formal arrangements and staff seem to 'catch' the message about what to wear through observation of others. This does seem hit and miss and in many ways this potentially difficult issue would be eased greatly if schools were open about what exactly is acceptable and what isn't.

If you have not been given any guidance at all, these ideas may help:

- Wear something 'safe' on your first day – in other words, no denim, nothing too short (just above the knee is as far as you should go), too tight, too revealing or too alternative. When you have been there for a while and have observed what other staff members wear you will be able to adapt your choices as necessary.
- Think about the impact that the colours you wear have on the pupils you work with. Research has been done on the psychology

of colour, showing that colours such as red are associated with danger and passion while green is associated with calm and rest. You can find out more about colour psychology by doing a search on the internet.

- Aim to be comfortable. As a TA you are likely to be involved in all kinds of activities throughout the school day, standing up, bending down, crouching by a desk, sitting on the floor, spending time outside and so on. The clothes that you wear have to allow you to do all these things in comfort.

It is perfectly acceptable to ask your headteacher if the school has a dress code or if there is anything that you should be aware of when planning what to wear for work. It's always better to ask a question like this than to feel that you have made a mistake on your first day by wearing the 'wrong' thing.

Will I have to perform first aid at school?

No, not unless you are a qualified first aider and are given that as one of your specific responsibilities. That said, there may be occasions when you have to administer first aid while waiting for the designated first aider to arrive, for example, to comfort an injured child or to stem a flow of blood. You will need to use your professional judgement in these situations.

It is important to know exactly what the expectations are of you regarding first aid. Your headteacher will be able to explain these. Make sure, too, that you know who in the school is qualified to administer first aid.

You can find out about first aid courses in your area from the British Red Cross First Aid Training website: www.redcrossfirstaid training.co.uk or from the St John Ambulance website: www.sja. org.uk.

When I start work as a TA will I have any say over how the classroom is organised?

No, this will be down to the class teacher. That said, there may be occasions when your advice is sought if it becomes necessary to rearrange the room due to pupil behaviour or for the purposes of a particular activity.

When you first get to know the classroom you are working in, pay particular attention to the following:

- the extent of the teaching space available (this may not be contained in a room, but may be open plan or spill out into corridor space or shared space between two classrooms)
- the way in which the furniture is arranged
- the display facilities and where these are located
- the main storage facilities and how these are managed and maintained.

This will enable you to make the best use of the space available to you and to form an opinion on any improvements that could be made. If you have any concerns in this area, discuss the use of space with the teacher(s) you work with.

I know that most teachers join a union before starting work in a school. Should TAs join a union too? If so, which one?

Absolutely! Unions can offer workers a range of support and advice and, while it is hoped that you will not need to call on your union during your working life, many TAs have been grateful for the support they have received at times of need. The union that most TAs join is UNISON. It has listed ten reasons to join a union as follows (these reasons are not all specific to schools as a place of work, but are general to the range of workplaces typically covered by UNISON):

- *You can earn more* – year on year, UNISON wins pay rises for its members. Average earnings are around 8 per cent higher in unionised workplaces.
- *You're more likely to get equal pay* – UNISON is campaigning to bring women's pay into line with men's. Workplaces with union recognition are 20 per cent more likely to have an equal opportunities policy.
- *You get more holiday* – UNISON has won increased leave for many of its members wherever they work.
- *You get more and better training* – UNISON provides courses to help you learn new skills, improve existing ones and develop your career. Since 1994 UNISON has won agreements with employers to pay for courses and provide time off for employees to attend them.
- *You get more maternity leave or parental leave* – if you belong to UNISON, your employer is more likely to have parental leave policies that are more generous than the statutory minimum.
- *You're less likely to be injured at work* – UNISON health and safety stewards are trained to minimise the risk of workplace injuries and ensure that employers meet their legal obligations.
- *If you do get injured at work, you'll get better compensation* – UNISON wins millions in legal compensation for people who are injured or become ill at work. UNISON won over £37 million in 2004 for members and their families.
- *You're less likely to be discriminated against* – UNISON campaigns for tougher laws to make it illegal to discriminate on the basis of sex, race, age, disability or sexual orientation. Black and Asian trade unionists earn 32 per cent more than non-unionised colleagues.
- *You can help keep our public services public* – UNISON campaigns against all forms of privatisation, including private finance initiative (PFI) and foundation hospitals. Where members have been transferred to the private sector UNISON has won them pay and employment protections.

- *You're less likely to be sacked* – trade union members are only half as likely to be sacked as non-members.

Some of the benefits of joining UNISON include the following:

- unrivalled protection and representation at work
- help with pay and conditions of service
- health and safety guidance and support
- confidential welfare services for you and your dependants in difficult times
- legal services including free help with work problems and legal support for members and their families
- pensions advice
- a special hotline, UNISONdirect, for help and advice on workplace issues
- online employment and workplace advice
- education and training advice and courses, leading to vocational and professional qualifications
- cash benefits for accidents and injuries at work
- a colour magazine sent to your home four times a year, a fortnightly newspaper for stewards and activists and a full range of publicity
- special deals on everything from computers, tax returns, holidays, mortgages, car breakdown services, insurance and credit cards
- access to a holiday centre for members and families at the Devon seaside.

It is not a legal requirement to join a union, but it is strongly advised. Make sure that if you do join a union you are absolutely clear about the benefits that you are entitled to and any limitations there may be on when you can start accessing them.

You can find out more about joining a union from the Trades Union Congress (TUC) website: www.tuc.org.uk, which lists all the unions and valuable information about pay, working hours and rights at work among other things. The UNISON website can be found here: www.unison.org.uk. It has an enquiry line that is open 6 a.m.–midnight Monday–Friday and 9 a.m.–4 p.m. on Saturdays: 0845 355 0845.

I've heard that newly qualified teachers (NQTs) have an induction period. Will I have one of those too?

Not necessarily. There is no statutory induction period as there is for NQTs but some schools do offer all new staff an induction into the workings of the school and the employee's job in particular. It is incredibly useful to undergo this kind of induction as you will find out all about the school's policies and practices. Undoubtedly it takes more than this brief induction fully to understand what makes a school tick but without this kind of basic introduction you can feel isolated very quickly.

You can find out from the headteacher if you are going to be given an induction into the workings of the school. If you are not, make sure that you have been told at least the following:

- who your line manager is (the person you report to directly)
- the legal responsibilities of TAs in the school (in particular regarding health and safety and child protection)
- where you can find the school staff handbook
- where school policies are kept and how you can access them
- the timings of the school day
- where the classrooms that you will be working in can be found
- where you can read the school's policies, particularly on SEN and behaviour

- where you can leave your coat and bag in safety
- where the toilets and staffroom are located
- where you can park or secure your bicycle
- where the school offices are and who the key administrative staff are
- where the facilities you will be expected to make use of in the course of your job can be found (reprographics, IT and so on).

Don't expect that you have to retain all this information having been told only once. You are bound to need to take time to settle in. The first few weeks may seem like a blur but in no time you'll feel like you belong.

Will I be entitled to use the staffroom?

Yes, almost certainly. It would be a very unusual school that prevented its TAs from using the staffroom facilities. You should be welcomed into the staffroom like any other member of staff, and be told exactly what the staffroom etiquette is. This may include contributing financially to drink and biscuit funds, helping to keep the staffroom kitchen area clean and tidy and so on. Whatever the protocol for your staffroom is, it should be explained to you so that you can fit in as easily as possible.

Will I have somewhere in the school for internal post?

You will most likely have a pigeonhole somewhere in the school that may or may not be shared with other TAs. This is so that internal (and external) communications can be put there when you are not on the premises or are working. If you are given one, sort through it regularly; you don't want to miss out on something important!

Should I expect the class teacher I am working with to tell me specifically what I am expected to do?

Yes it would be appropriate to expect this. Right from the first day, communication between you and the teacher should be clear and you should be left in no doubt as to what you should be doing with your time in the school.

Some teachers go so far as to give TAs a checklist for each lesson or session. This includes information such as the following:

- the key points of learning that are intended
- the resources required to deliver the lesson
- where the resources can be found and what resources the TA would be expected to use
- whether any resources need to be booked in advance (for example, a room, TV or computer)
- whether any resources need to be created or developed
- the timings of the lesson or session.

Do not be surprised if this kind of arrangement is not in place in your school, but something similar should be, even if it is simply verbal. A teacher would not be making the most of his/her TA without sharing information of this kind in advance of a lesson or session.

If I am employed to work with a specific pupil (or pupils), for example, those with particular learning needs, should I not help other pupils in the class?

You will determine the best way for you to work most effectively through discussion with the class teacher but as a rule of thumb it is worth keeping in mind that you should support all the pupils you come into contact with. Even if you are there in the classroom to support one child who, through inclusion, has been integrated into the mainstream but who has specific needs, you will inevitably come across other pupils who perhaps are working with the child you are supporting and who may require your assistance. The core spirit of the role is such that you would support all those in need that you encounter, whilst bearing in mind the purpose for which you are employed at the school.

> If you are in any doubt about this, talk to the teacher(s) you work with for clarity.

If I am employed to work with a child with SEN who would my line manager be, the special educational needs coordinator (SENCO) or the teacher?

Your job will entail you giving support to the teacher and the SENCO through your work with the child, but ultimately it is most likely that your line manager would be the class teacher. There are no hard and fast rules about this though, and it would all depend on the way in which your school is structured. As well as having a line manager, there is also likely to be a member of the school's senior leadership team (sometimes called a senior management team) who will have responsibilities for support staff in the school. All of this should be made clear to you when you start, and if anything needs clarifying, don't hesitate to ask.

How do I find out about the special needs of any children I work with? Do they have files I should read?

You should be told all you need to know by the class teacher and the SENCO. They will supply the relevant documents for you to read and will point you in the right direction for further information on the condition affecting the child or children. While you would not be expected to become an expert in these conditions or needs, doing some additional background reading will undoubtedly lead to enhanced job satisfaction and a better quality of support for the children.

Schools are required to keep a curricular record on each pupil. The curricular record is designed to record a pupil's academic achievements, other skills, abilities and progress in school. The records must be updated at least once each year.

In addition to the curricular record, schools must also keep an educational record that contains additional and necessary information about the child. The educational record contains any statement of SEN held in respect of the child and any personal education plan (PEP).

> Your headteacher will be able to tell you all you need to know about the records held in respect of the pupils at your school.

What are PEPs? Does every child have one?

PEPs are personal education plans which all looked after children should have (those children 'looked after' by the local authority). These plans help to ensure access to services and support and to contribute to stability for the child. Not every child has a PEP.

PEPs are not the same as individual education plans (IEPs) although there are similarities between them. Children with SEN typically have an IEP and these are usually reviewed twice a year. IEPs set out:

- the short-term targets set for or by the child
- the teaching strategies to be used
- the provision to be put in place
- when the plan is to be reviewed
- success and/or exit criteria
- outcomes (to be recorded when the IEP is reviewed).

It is important to understand fully what the arrangements are for pupils with SEN in your school. You can find out more about SEN from TeacherNet: www.teachernet.gov.uk, where you can also download the SEN Code of Practice. You should also have a read of your school's SEN policy.

I understand that I might be asked to help clean up a child after incidents and accidents. I appreciate that CPIs are crucially important but how can I protect myself from false accusations?

It is likely that you will be involved in cleaning up a child at some stage and you may even be supporting a child with continence issues. Any personal care of a child puts the carer at potential risk but your school will have procedures set up to cover this.

In some schools, the fact that you will have been CRB checked is enough by way of protection whereas other schools will always ensure that there are two members of staff present when undertaking any personal care of children.

Before you start work in a school make sure you discuss with the headteacher what the arrangements are for such incidents taking place. If you are at all unsure about these procedures, ask for clarification and if you still have uncertainties about how effectively you will be protected, talk to your union. It is important to know what the expectations of you are, and it is equally important to feel that these are reasonable and safe.

The names of year groups have changed since I was at school. How can I find out what they mean now?

There are four key stages of the National Curriculum plus the Foundation Stage. These are set out in Table 3.1.

Table 3.1

Key stage	Year groups	Ages
1	1–2	5–7
2	3–6	7–11
3	7–9	11–14
4	10–11	14–16

As a rough guide, if you add 5 to the year group you get the age of the children in it. For example, the children in year 8 are around the age of 13.

The Foundation Stage was introduced in September 2000 for children aged 3–5. It covers nursery and reception classes.

> You can find out more about the key stages of the National Curriculum and the Foundation Stage from the QCA website: www.qca.org.uk.

Where can I find out more about the National Curriculum?

You can find the full National Curriculum online, along with explanatory notes and guidance. In short, the National Curriculum, combined with religious education, collective worship, sex and relationship education and careers education, comprises all the learning and other experiences that a school provides for its pupils.

The reason we have a National Curriculum is, according to TeacherNet, 'to secure for all pupils, irrespective of social background, culture, race, gender, differences in ability and disabilities, an entitlement to a number of areas of learning'. The Curriculum has a statutory inclusion statement outlining how teachers can modify the Curriculum to provide all pupils with challenging work at each key stage.

The Foundation Stage sets out six areas of learning that form the basis of the curriculum for children aged 3–5. These areas of learning are:

- Personal, social and emotional development
- Communication, language and literacy
- Mathematical development
- Knowledge and understanding of the world
- Physical development
- Creative development

You can find out more about the subjects included in the National Curriculum from the following website: www.curriculumonline. gov.uk.

CHAPTER 4

All about workload

Pleasure in the job puts perfection in the work.

(Aristotle)

Introduction

We hear so much in the media and in schools about teachers' work-loads that we might be forgiven for thinking that this group is the only one in schools juggling multiple tasks in limited time. The reality of school life is that many others within the school community are grappling with demanding workloads (pupils included), and staying on top of it and in control can be a challenge in itself.

Recognising and acknowledging the extent of your role and the ways in which you can manage your workload goes a long way towards becoming as efficient as possible in your job, not to mention increasing your chances of reaping genuine enjoyment from your work. And that has to be an essential goal!

This chapter explores some of the likely tasks and responsibilities that TAs will face in their work and ideas on how to manage and balance workload.

FAQs in this chapter cover:

- Likely tasks TAs are asked to do
- The '25 tasks'
- Additional tasks
- The respective roles of teachers and TAs
- Planning and preparing for lessons
- Feeding back to teachers
- Behaviour management
- Target setting
- Prioritising work
- Time management
- Procrastination
- Workload stress
- Staff meetings
- School visits

What are the likely tasks I will be asked to do as a TA?

The best way of identifying these is to explore the National Occupational Standards for TAs (see also page 5). Each standard has a list of performance indicators that help to outline exactly the kinds of tasks that TAs are typically involved in.

Below are the standards at NVQ/SVQ Levels 2 and 3 and the units that they are organised into, with examples of the kind of tasks that TAs engage in to demonstrate that they are meeting the standards. Use these to gain a clear idea of the kinds of tasks you would do as a TA in a school (remember that it is highly unlikely that you would be undertaking *all* these tasks). Table 4.1 has been included by way of *example*.

Table 4.1

Unit	Standards	Example tasks
2-1: Help with classroom resources and records	2-1.1 Help with organisation of the learning environment 2-1.2 Help with classroom records	• Set out learning materials as instructed by the teacher • Check the condition of learning materials after use • Update pupil records under the teacher's direction • Collect, collate and pass on as promptly as possible information for the school office
2-2: Help with the care and support of pupils	2-2.1 Help with the care and support of individual pupils 2-2.2 Help with the care and support of groups of pupils	• Provide pupils with individual care as specified by the teacher • Provide comfort and immediate care for minor accidents and upsets and report all serious problems to the relevant people • Respond to conflict situations and anti-social behaviour in line with school policies • Demonstrate respect for the rights of others through your own interactions with pupils and adults
2-3: Provide support for learning activities	2-3.1 Support the teacher in the planning and evaluation of learning activities 2-3.2 Support the delivery of learning activities	• Offer constructive suggestions on the kind of support you can offer for a planned activity • Offer the teacher constructive feedback on the activity • Provide support to enable pupils to follow instructions • Use praise, commentary and assistance to encourage pupils to stay on task

continued on next page

Table 4.1 continued

Unit	Standards	Example tasks
2-4: Provide effective support for your colleagues	2-4.1 Maintain working relationships with colleagues 2-4.2 Develop your effectiveness in a support role	• Provide consistent and effective support for colleagues in line with the responsibilities of your role • Communicate openly and honestly with colleagues • Undertake agreed development actions within the required timescale • Make effective use of the development support available to you
2-5: Support literacy and numeracy activities in the classroom	2-5.1 Help pupils with activities that develop literacy skills 2-5.2 Help pupils with activities that develop numeracy skills	• Give encouragement and feedback using language and vocabulary which the pupil can understand • Obtain up-to-date information from the teacher on: – the learning objectives of the activity – the type of support you are to give – the teacher's expectations of the pupil's current literacy skills • Provide the teacher with relevant feedback on the progress of the activity and the pupil's response to it • Offer the required types of support as and when needed by the pupil

3-1: Contribute to the management of pupil behaviour	3-1.1 Promote school policies with regard to pupil behaviour 3-1.2 Support the implementation of strategies to manage pupil behaviour	• Encourage pupils to take responsibility for their own behaviour • Recognise uncharacteristic behaviour patterns in individual pupils and report these promptly to the appropriate person • Promptly report any problems in implementing agreed strategies to the teacher • Provide feedback to teachers on progress made by any pupils with a behaviour support plan
3-2: Establish and maintain relationships with individual pupils and groups	3-2.1 Establish and maintain relationships with individual pupils 3-2.2 Establish and maintain relationships with groups of pupils	• Provide levels of individual attention, reassurance and help as appropriate to a pupil's needs • Monitor the pupil's response to your interactions and, where necessary, modify your approach to ensure the desired outcomes are achieved • Demonstrate your valuing of and interest in the group through your body language, attentiveness and use of language • Encourage the group to take responsibility for their own interactions and social cohesion

continued on next page

Table 4.1 continued

Unit	Standards	Example tasks
3-3: Support pupils during learning activities	3-3.1 Provide support for learning activities 3-3.2 Promote independent learning	• Clarify and confirm with the teacher your role in supporting pupils engaged in learning activities • Provide support as needed to enable pupils to follow instructions • Provide information, advice and opportunities for pupils to choose and make decisions about their own learning • Help pupils to review their learning strategies and achievements and plan for future learning
3-4: Review and develop your own professional practice	3-4.1 Review your own professional practice 3-4.2 Develop your professional practice	• Recognise the different ways in which the role you play contributes to raising pupil achievement • Form realistic judgements about how well your own practice matches expectations about competent performance in all aspects of the contribution you make • Seek and make good use of development opportunities available to you within your employment context • Review and update your personal development objectives on a regular basis to reflect progress made and any new and changing expectations about your role

3-5: Assist in preparing and maintaining the learning environment	3-5.1 Help prepare the learning environment 3-5.2 Prepare learning materials for use 3-5.3 Monitor and maintain the learning environment	• Check the availability and location of safety equipment in the learning environment • Have the learning environment ready for use when needed • Confirm the type and quantity of materials needed with the teacher • Take steps to keep any wastage of materials to a minimum • Adjust lighting, ventilation and, where possible, heating to ensure the comfort of pupils and adults and to comply with health and safety requirements • Encourage pupils to return equipment and materials to the appropriate place after use
3-6: Contribute to maintaining pupil records	3-6.1 Contribute to maintaining pupil records 3-6.2 Contribute to maintaining the record-keeping system	• Confirm your role and responsibilities for helping to maintain pupil records with the teacher • Ensure that your agreed contributions to pupil records are accurate, complete and up to date • Comply with the school requirements for storage and security of pupil records at all times • Contribute to reviewing the record-keeping system when required

continued on next page

Table 4.1 continued

Unit	Standards	Example tasks
3-7: Observe and report on pupil performance	3-7.1 Observe pupil performance 3-7.2 Report on pupil performance	• Clarify and confirm the reasons and objectives for observing pupils' performance with the teacher • Use facilitative techniques that are consistent with the objectives of the observations • Present evidence that accurately reflects the information gained from your observations and recordings • Observe school policies and procedures for confidentiality of information about pupils
3-8: Contribute to the planning and evaluation of learning activities	3-8.1 Contribute to the planning of learning activities 3-8.2 Contribute to the evaluation of learning activities	• Give constructive and timely feedback on ideas and options being explored • Confirm your understanding of your contribution to implementing the plan with the teacher • Express a realistic and fair view on the success of the learning activities taking account of the agreed success measures • Deal with any differences of opinion in a way that maintains effective working relationships with colleagues

3-9: Promote pupils' social and emotional development	3-9.1 Support pupils in developing relationships with others 3-9.2 Contribute to pupils' development of self-reliance and self-esteem 3-9.3 Contribute to pupils' ability to recognise and deal with emotions	• Interact with pupils and other adults in ways that provide a positive and consistent example of effective working relationships • Encourage pupils to resolve minor conflicts amicably and safely • Listen carefully to pupils and encourage them to communicate their needs and ideas • Make effective use of opportunities for pupils to develop self-help skills • Interact with pupils in a manner that encourages and supports them in expressing and dealing with emotions in a socially acceptable manner • Deal with emotional outbursts and negative reactions in a calm and reassuring manner and in line with school policy
3-10: Support the maintenance of pupil safety and security	3-10.1 Contribute to the maintenance of a safe and secure learning environment 3-10.2 Minimise the risks arising from health emergencies	• Maintain the learning environment as safe and as free from hazards as possible during work activities • Implement appropriate safety and security procedures without delay in an emergency • Provide the individual with the health emergency with support, both verbally and by physical presence • Offer appropriate support to any others involved in the incident once the initial danger is passed

continued on next page

Table 4.1 continued

Unit	Standards	Example tasks
3-11: Contribute to the health and well-being of pupils	3-11.1 Support pupils in adjusting to a new setting 3-11.2 Support pupils in maintaining standards of health and hygiene 3-11.3 Respond to signs of health problems	• Contribute to strategies designed to help pupils join in activities and adjust to the setting • Positively encourage other pupils to interact with and welcome new arrivals • Provide advice and assistance as required to enable pupils to develop basic hygiene skills • Assist pupils to access appropriate medical and health care when needed • Recognise and respond promptly to changes in behaviour and well-being that are signs of common illnesses in children and young people • Recognise the signs of mental or emotional distress and respond in a manner consistent with your role and school policies and procedures
3-12: Provide support for bilingual/ multilingual pupils	3-12.1 Support development of the target language 3-12.2 Help bilingual/ multilingual pupils to access the curriculum	• Provide opportunities for the pupils to interact with yourself and others using their knowledge of the target language • Utilise opportunities to model the target language for the pupils and to scaffold their learning of the target language

- Utilise pupils' previous knowledge and experience to encourage their active involvement in learning activities
- Use praise and constructive feedback to maintain pupils' interest in the learning activities

3-13: Support pupils with communication and interaction difficulties	3-13.1 Enable pupils with communication and interaction difficulties to participate in learning activities 3-13.2 Help pupils with communication and interaction difficulties to develop relationships with others	• Obtain detailed information from the teacher about the planned learning tasks and activities • Help pupils to make effective use of augmented and alternative means of communication as appropriate to their needs • Provide opportunities for pupils with communication and interaction difficulties to initiate, respond to and maintain relationships with others • Respond to the pupils' level of expressive and receptive language to reinforce spoken language and to promote autonomy
3-14: Support pupils with cognition and learning difficulties	3-14.1 Support pupils with cognition and learning difficulties during learning activities	• Obtain accurate up-to-date information about the pupils' cognition and learning needs • Promptly report any problems in supporting pupils during learning activities to the teacher

continued on next page

Table 4.1 continued

Unit	Standards	Example tasks
	3-14.2 Help pupils with cognition and learning difficulties to develop effective learning strategies	• Use specific visual, auditory and tactile methods to help pupils understand the functional use of objects and gain information about the environment • Give positive encouragement, feedback and praise to reinforce and sustain pupils' interest and efforts in learning activities
3-15: Support pupils with behavioural, emotional and social development needs	3-15.1 Support the behaviour management of pupils with behavioural, emotional and social development needs 3-15.2 Help pupils with behavioural, emotional and social development needs to develop relationships with others 3-15.3 Help pupils with behavioural, emotional and social development needs to develop self-reliance and self-esteem	• Provide an effective role model for the standards of behaviour expected of pupils and adults within the school • Encourage pupils to take responsibility for their own behaviour • Encourage pupils to resolve minor conflicts amicably and safely • Respond appropriately to conflict situations and incidents of anti-social behaviour with due consideration for your own safety and that of others • Listen carefully to pupils and help them to communicate their needs and ideas • Make effective use of opportunities for pupils to develop self-management skills

3-16: Provide support for pupils with sensory and/or physical impairment	3-16.1 Enable pupils with sensory and/or physical impairment to participate in learning activities 3-16.2 Implement structured learning programmes for pupils with sensory and/or physical impairment	• Adapt the learning environment and materials, as agreed with the teacher, to enable pupils with sensory and/or physical impairment to participate in the planned learning tasks and activities • Use teaching and learning materials in the appropriate medium as directed by the teacher • Jointly and cooperatively plan and agree the structured learning programme with the relevant people • Ensure that the timing and location of the structured activities minimises distractions to the pupil and disruptions to the normal routines and schedules
3-17: Support the use of ICT in the classroom	3-17.1 Prepare ICT equipment for use in the classroom 3-17.2 Support classroom use of ICT equipment	• Confirm the requirements for ICT equipment with the teacher • Make sure that there is ready access to accessories, consumables and information needed to use the equipment effectively • Operate ICT equipment correctly and safely when asked to do so • Monitor the safe use of equipment by others and intervene promptly where actions may be dangerous

continued on next page

Table 4.1 continued

Unit	Standards	Example tasks
3-18: Help pupils to develop their literacy skills	3-18.1 Help pupils to develop their reading skills 3-18.2 Help pupils to develop their writing skills 3-18.3 Help pupils to develop their speaking and listening skills	• Agree the support strategies to be used with individual and groups of pupils • Obtain the resources needed to implement the agreed support strategies • Clarify and confirm your understanding of the pupils' learning needs with the teacher • Implement the agreed strategies correctly to support development of the pupils' writing skills • Provide opportunities for pupils to engage in conversation, discussion and questioning • Create opportunities to extend pupils' understanding about the importance of attentive listening and taking turns to speak
3-19: Help pupils to develop their numeracy skills	3-19.1 Help pupils to develop their understanding and use of numbers 3-19.2 Help pupils to understand and use shape, space and measures	• Agree which pupils you will be working with and how this will be organised in relation to what the teacher and other pupils will be doing • Use praise and assistance appropriately to maintain the pupils' interest in using numbers

- Deal with difficulties in understanding and using shape, space and measures in ways that maintain the pupils' confidence and self-esteem
- Monitor progress towards the intended learning outcomes and provide feedback to the pupils in a manner appropriate to their age and achievements

3-20: Help pupils to access the curriculum	3-20.1 Provide literacy support to help pupils to access the curriculum 3-20.2 Provide numeracy support to help pupils to access the curriculum	• Clarify and confirm your understanding of the literacy demands and objectives of the learning activities planned by the teacher • Monitor the pupils' progress in developing literacy skills and, if relevant, modify the type and level of literacy support provided • Use appropriate strategies to provide the agreed numeracy support during the planned learning activities • Deal with difficulties in coping with the numeracy demands of learning activities in ways that maintain the pupils' confidence and self-esteem

continued on next page

Table 4.1 continued

Unit	Standards	Example tasks
3-21: Support the development and effectiveness of work teams	3-21.1 Contribute to effective team practice 3-21.2 Contribute to the development of the work team	• Work in ways that conform to decisions taken by the team • Offer help and advice to colleagues when they ask for it, when this is consistent with your other responsibilities • Contribute effectively to the review of team practice • Recognise and value the strengths that each team member brings to a situation
3-22: Develop and maintain working relationships with other professionals	3-22.1 Work effectively with other professionals 3-22.2 Maintain effective working relationships with other professionals	• Interact with other professionals in a manner likely to promote trust and confidence in the relationship • Refer matters beyond your competence, role and responsibility to the relevant individuals within the school • Share information that is complete, accurate and within the boundaries of your knowledge and responsibilities • Clearly explain any factors limiting your ability to cooperate

3-23: Liaise effectively with parents	3-23.1 Share information with parents about their children 3-23.2 Share the care of children with their parents	• Refer requests for information beyond your role and responsibility to the relevant person • Promptly report any difficulties in communicating with parents to the relevant person • Care for children in ways that have regard to their home values and practices and their parents' expressed wishes, and are consistent with the policies and procedures of the school • Give positive reassurance in response to parents' concerns and anxieties about their children

I have heard that there are 25 tasks that TAs now have to do instead of teachers. Is this the case?

No, not entirely. There is a list of 25 tasks that were once performed typically by teachers, but that now should not routinely be done by them. Other support staff in a school can undertake these tasks, not necessarily only TAs. This is as a result of the National Workload Agreement for teachers (see page 8) and the development of the roles of school support staff.

The list of 25 tasks that need not be carried out by teachers now is as follows:

- collecting money
- chasing absences
- bulk photocopying
- copy typing
- producing standard letters
- producing class lists

- record keeping and filing
- classroom display
- analysing attendance figures
- processing exam results
- collating pupil reports
- administering work experience
- administering examinations
- invigilating examinations
- administering teacher cover
- ICT troubleshooting and minor repairs
- commissioning new ICT equipment
- ordering supplies and equipment
- stocktaking
- cataloguing, preparing, issuing and maintaining equipment and materials
- minuting meetings
- coordinating and submitting bids
- seeking and giving personnel advice
- managing pupil data
- inputting pupil data.

It is likely that TAs would be asked to undertake at least some of the above tasks in schools. Find out more about how these tasks have been distributed in your school from your headteacher.

Are there any extra tasks I am likely to be asked to undertake?

There may well be additional tasks not specified in your job description that you are asked to contribute towards. These can really help to cement you in the school and help you to feel a valued part of the school community. On the other hand, being asked to perform above and beyond the call of duty can also result in feeling put upon so it's important to be aware of how you respond to additional requests for your involvement. Of course, you may decide that you want to offer your services if you perceive that the school has a particular need.

Additional tasks that you may be involved in include:

- working with a particular group of pupils such as school refusers or those with English as a second or additional language
- working with colleagues in schools the pupils you support are moving to, for example, when they move from primary to secondary school or from the mainstream to a special needs school
- communicating with parents (normally this would be done by the teacher you are working with but there may be occasions when it is appropriate for you to do this)
- getting involved with specific behaviour support programmes, particularly if working with a child who has behaviour issues or if the school is going through the process of implementing a whole school approach to tackling bad behaviour
- providing first aid (only if qualified to do so)
- working with pupils who are deemed to be gifted and talented
- mentoring other TAs
- using additional skills that you have that may be needed by the school – for example, language skills or musical skills.

What is the most important thing to remember about the respective roles of teachers and TAs?

In short, the functions of teachers and TAs are very different. Teachers plan lessons, direct learning in the classroom and assess pupil progress among other things. TAs support teachers in performing these roles, working sometimes independently with pupils but invariably under the direction of the class teacher. The roles are inextricably linked, but distinct in their own rights.

Is it right to expect that my role in the classroom will be taken into consideration by the teacher when he/she plans lessons?

Absolutely! Your presence in the classroom should be fully planned for by the teacher so that your skills can be utilised to maximum effect for the pupils. You should also be given adequate and appropriate space in which to undertake any of the tasks expected of you.

It is also worth keeping in mind that the teacher(s) you work with should be ensuring that you know precisely what the purpose of each lesson activity is. If at any time you don't know, make sure you ask. Without this knowledge, it will be impossible to facilitate the full participation of all the pupils you work with.

Will I be asked to undertake any planning of lessons as a TA?

You may be asked to do this, but only under the supervision of the class teacher. It is in fact very useful for TAs to be involved to some extent in the planning of work for classes. This may simply be in the form of a quick discussion between teacher and TA to ensure that both know exactly what the learning intentions for the day/lesson are. For the medium-term planning (for, say, half a term), you may be involved in longer discussions with the class teacher and it could well be appropriate for you to undertake some planning for one particular child or a small group of children but this would only usually be done under the supervision of the teacher.

Planning is a crucial aspect of work in the classroom and although it is ultimately the teacher's responsibility, it is important for TAs to be informed, whether they undertake small aspects of planning tasks or not.

Some schools adopt a so-called 'virtuous circle' of planning, pre-paring, doing and reviewing. This is a useful model to follow as it recognises that each lesson delivered needs to be planned for, prepared for, carried out and reviewed. Planning, therefore, is not an isolated aspect of the job, but part of an extended sequence of events.

Although the teacher I work with does most of the planning, I am often involved in preparing for lessons. Is this OK?

Absolutely! There are bound to be aspects of the lessons planned for that need to be prepared and this is just the kind of task that teachers ask their TAs to help out with.

When you are working closely with a teacher and you have developed a strong working relationship, you will naturally fall into an effective planning and preparing 'system'. At first this may take much discussion between you but over time you will know each other's ways of working and tasks will be covered effectively and efficiently utilising your combined skills to best outcomes. Well, that's the idea! And your involvement in planning and preparation is key.

I know that I should be feeding back to the teacher I'm working with. What's the best way of doing this?

It's always best to feedback in person as soon as possible after a lesson. There won't always be much to say but there will usually be at least a word or two that should be said about the progress and behaviour of the children you are working with. However, there is not always the time or space in which to do this immediately after a lesson, session or day. Other demands on the teacher's time or on your time can mean that this kind of useful, immediate feedback is delayed, decreasing its value. If you find that this is happening more often than not, this is something to discuss with the teacher(s) you work with. You may also want to start using a notebook in which you can communicate with the teacher in writing on the occasions when you haven't been able to speak. This is a useful last resort though, and should not be relied on all the time. There is no replacement for verbal communication between a teacher and his/her TA.

Would I ever be responsible for behaviour management?

As a TA working in a classroom with a teacher, no, you won't ever have sole responsibility for behaviour management; that will be the teacher's responsibility. That said, you will be responsible for *supporting* the teacher and helping to ensure that the school's behaviour management policy is adhered to.

When working with an individual or a small group of pupils, you will be responsible for ensuring that behaviour was in line with the teacher's expectations. It is acceptable for you to reprimand when necessary (in line with the teacher's policy for dealing with behaviour issues in his/her classroom) just as it is acceptable to ask for assistance from the teacher should behaviour get out of hand.

Make sure that you know exactly what your school's behaviour management policy says, and precisely how the teacher you are working with interprets it. It is essential that all the adults in a classroom are absolutely clear and united on this.

How can I best set targets for myself when I'm organising my work? Surely it's better if I just get on with it?

You're right, you could 'just get on with it' but we do know from research that people who set themselves goals and targets do tend to achieve more than those who do not. There are bound to be aspects of your work that you can develop or that would simply benefit from the greater degree of organisation that goal or target setting encourages.

When you do set yourself goals or targets, these pointers may help:

- Think about goals in terms of being for the short, medium or long term. For example, there may be tasks that you need to complete within the next hour, while others are goals for the term or half term and others may be in place for the year.
- Set goals for yourself that are achievable. That sounds obvious but it is incredibly common for people not to do this with the inevitable outcome of failure.
- Discuss your goal setting with the teacher you work with just to ensure that your priorities are shared.
- Allow yourself to acknowledge what you achieve.

How can I prioritise my work when I am there to assist a teacher?

There will inevitably be some aspects of your work that you can prioritise despite the fact that you are there to assist the teacher and will therefore be guided by what he/she needs you to achieve. The best way to focus on prioritising is to discuss with the teacher realistically what is of high importance, what is moderately important and what is of low importance. In order to be effective you can only achieve one thing at a time so, in the absence of any precise guidance from the teacher, go for the high priority tasks first.

I would really like to improve my time management skills but I don't really know where to start. What can I do for myself?

First of all you are not alone! Time management is the kind of skill it can take a lifetime to learn and at any given moment we all could profitably focus on our use of time.

When focusing on time management do remember that you are unlikely ever to reach the end of the 'list'. There will nearly always be something else that could be done and that is the nature of the job. If you only derive satisfaction from getting everything done, you may have to alter your perspective for when you are working in a school!

Time management is partly about understanding how you work best. Some like to plod away at a steady pace while others thrive on bursts of intense activity followed by periods of lower productivity. Both approaches are equally valid but if you're a natural steady plodder and you try to push yourself into working in intense bursts you're unlikely to thrive. The key is to organise your work in such a way as to accommodate your natural propensities.

These ideas may help you to explore your time management skills:

- Be realistic – as far as is possible – about what you can achieve in any given time. Take possible interruptions into account.
- Split what you have to achieve into prioritised goals.
- Write lists if that helps you to keep on top of what needs doing.
- Make sure you work in as tidy a space as possible.
- Aim to do tasks that allow it in a place where you won't be interrupted.
- Take some time to consider whether there are any tasks you routinely do that could be consolidated or cut out altogether. Discuss any conclusions you reach with the teacher(s) you work with.
- Aim to be aware of the schedules that exist in your school, for example, when reports are due, any specific termly events such as concerts or school visits and so on. Make sure that you know the impact these events will have on your workload.
- Collaborate with other TAs and teachers as much as possible. There is no point in redoing something that has already been created and is known to work well. Always share burdens of work in schools wherever possible.

I know I have a tendency to procrastinate, especially when I have more than a couple of tasks to do. What can I do about this?

You're not the only one affected by procrastination – it must surely affect every one of us at some time or other. It is important to be respectful of your natural ebbs and flows in energy. Some days you will be more inclined to tackle just about anything and other days everything may seem like a monumental chore. We all have natural slump times and action times. The trick is to blast through the slumps if we feel that procrastination is stealing our time. These ideas may help:

- While it may be appropriate to put off a task temporarily, don't do this indefinitely. What you don't get done today should have a place in your schedule for the next time you are in school.
- If a particular task is becoming a source of stress aim to talk to the teacher you work with about it and plan to do something towards it sooner rather than later. Everything starts with one step, whatever size the task is.
- Learn to acknowledge any feelings of satisfaction you get on completing a task. Don't just whizz on to the next one. Pause and praise yourself, and remember that procrastination prevents you from achieving that feeling!

It is possible for everyone to improve their relationship with time. The results you get will depend on the effort you want to put in. If you feel that time management is a development issue for you make sure that you discuss this with the teacher(s) you work with as well as your headteacher if necessary. You may also want to take a look at the many books that exist on time management as well as the websites out there. Most of them cover procrastination too.

*I sometimes find myself getting stressed about
everything I have to achieve, especially if my
'to do' list has more than about five items on it.
There is always something unexpected that comes
up. How can I manage that?*

You're half way there in acknowledging that the unexpected always
seems to happen in schools! Especially as a TA, there will always
be incidents that you need to respond to and these are likely to
take you off course for part of each day. Life in school cannot be controlled and it is important not to forget that. You will cope better
with the uncertainty inherent in being part of a school community
by being resilient and flexible when it comes to your work and the
way in which you spend your time. Focus on one thing at a time
whenever possible and only pursue the distractions that are
absolutely vital. Then get back on track as soon as possible. If you
are flexible in your approach, you will not be overwhelmed. It may
be a well-worn phrase, but if you can 'go with the flow' school life
will far less stressful.

Should I have to attend staff meetings as a TA?

Attending staff meetings is a great way of finding out more about
how the school is run and how it makes decisions. There are, however,
financial implications of attending these meetings and these would
need to be discussed with your school. Check your contract carefully
to see what you are contracted to do. Anything that isn't contracted
(and therefore paid for) should be voluntary rather than compulsory.
If in any doubt about whether you should attend staff meetings, talk
to the headteacher.

Some schools arrange for TAs to be invited to all staff meetings,
without the expectation that they should attend them all. If there
are any meetings that you really should attend, or are required to
attend, the hours worked are either paid or time off is given in lieu.

Always check with your headteacher if you are unsure what your obligations are regarding attending meetings.

Will I be expected to go on school trips?

Most schools are fully committed to giving their pupils out-of-school experiences, whatever age they are. School trips and visits are a crucial element of curriculum enrichment and pupils benefit from them immeasurably in most cases. As a TA, you will almost certainly be asked to be involved in most if not all stages of a trip, from planning it to the actual day. The teacher(s) you work with will talk you through this process.

Your union is likely to have advice for its members who go on school trips so it would be worth checking to see if there is anything it has highlighted that you should be aware of.

CHAPTER 5

Working with children

It takes a village to raise a child.

(African proverb)

Introduction

As a TA you will be working closely with children, naturally, as well as with other adults. While many millions of words, several hundred books (if not more!) and countless articles have been written about how people can best work with children, bringing out the best in them and helping them to reach their potential, in my opinion, this all boils down to one word: relationships. The quality and resilience of the relationships that you build with the children you work with will help them to grow in their work and themselves as people. Developing effective working relationships is, therefore, crucial to the job.

Part of this process of relationship building entails using motivational techniques to bring out the best in each child. Unless motivated, there is little reason to achieve, or to produce work. Unless motivated, the best you can hope to achieve with the children you work with is stagnation. Mostly, these techniques will come naturally to you. After all, we are all used to motivating ourselves and can draw on this experience to help to motivate others.

This chapter explores how to go about building effective working relationships with young learners and how to motivate them into becoming the best they can be.

FAQs in this chapter cover:

- Developing healthy relationships with children
- Not getting on with a child
- Helping a child who is 'down'
- Encouraging pupils to try harder
- The importance of goals for young people
- Goal setting
- Giving a child feedback
- Equality issues in the classroom
- Recognising the efforts of each child
- Motivating pupils
- Time management skills for children

How can I develop strong and positive relationships with the children I work with?

You will find that this comes naturally, especially if you enjoy working with people (and presumably you do to be in the job!). Developing relationships is a key aspect of working in a school and this is achieved in all kinds of ways. These ideas may help:

- take the time to chat to pupils and take an interest in what they do outside school
- be aware of the opportunities that exist to raise pupils' self-esteem and self-respect
- be approachable and willing to listen to pupils when they need to talk
- be aware of friendship groups and of helping pupils to integrate more (without interfering!)
- take the opportunity to talk to pupils outside the classroom.

As long as you are aware that the opportunity to develop and improve the relationships you have with pupils is ever-present, you cannot fail. Every interaction you have with a child builds on those that have gone previously. At each meeting, there is the option to improve a relationship or to injure it. Make sure that you consciously make the right choice.

What if I have to work with a child who I really cannot get on with? What should I do?

You are as human as the rest of us and when interacting with a large number of young people there are bound to be one or two who touch a nerve or wind you up. It is always possible to improve your relationship with a child and to find the common ground between you. Try these ideas:

- Think about exactly what it is about the child that you have difficulty getting on with.
- Find out if other colleagues have the same difficulties that you do.
- Take the time to talk to the child about life in general, not just school work. Do you share any common interests? Does this help you to see a new side to the person?
- Ask the teacher you work with for ideas on relating to this child.
- Identify three things that you like about the child, for example, a quirky sense of humour, a cheeky smile, an independent streak, a strong sense of self and so on.
- Aim to determine whether there is anything in the child that you dislike that reminds you of yourself or someone else that you know.

Always remember that the *behaviour* is not the *person.* Separate the two and you will find it easier to maintain solid and effective working relationships with all you come into contact with. For a fuller discussion of this topic see Chapter 6.

What do I do if I observe that a child is not behaving in their usual way and if they are clearly 'down' and distracted?

There are bound to be times when you notice this in the children you work with as they are fully feeling and emotional beings. It is important to aim to find out what the cause might be but don't attack this head on. Take the opportunity to sit beside the child while he/she is working and ask them how they are. This will give you the chance to observe how they respond. If they start to open up, listen intently to what they say and see if you can offer immediate reassurance and peace of mind. If not, pass your observations on to the teacher and keep a close eye on the child over the next few weeks. If the child is not feeling well physically, go through the usual procedures in your school for taking care of poorly ones.

Don't let this go on indefinitely. If a child is clearly distressed in some way, or their behaviour has altered to such an extent that you have noticed, you and the teacher(s) you work with need to work out how you can support the child to get them back to their usual self. It may be that you raise your concerns with the child's parents or carers but this would be a decision for the teacher to take.

How can I encourage pupils to try harder with the work that is set for them? Sometimes they just don't want to know.

It's always worth talking to the teacher about any children that seem especially demotivated just in case there are underlying causes impacting on their work. This is exactly the kind of observation that should be passed on to teachers too, even if you know that he/she has already picked up on it. Every piece of additional information you can give as someone working with a child is valuable.

The basics of motivation lie in goal setting. Research has shown that deciding to pursue goals depends on two main factors:

- desirability (how attractive is the attainment of the goal?)
- feasibility (is there the belief that the goal can be achieved?).

In other words, the child needs to feel the goal is something worth reaching, and that he/she has a good chance of reaching it. If it's not worth it and feels like a mountain to climb anyway, most young learners would (perhaps rightly) think 'what's the point?'. That's where you come in! In order to motivate effectively, you need to help him/her to see and feel that the goal of completing the work is both desirable and feasible. Obviously the tactics you use to do this will depend on the task in hand, but whatever you do, make sure you help them to desire the goal and to think that they can achieve it. Remember, it's all about desirability and feasibility. That's how you move towards creating what is called intrinsic motivation (the kind of motivation children need to do things without external pressure or inducement). In other words, you are simply creating the circumstances in which their own internal motivation kicks in and he/she completes the task because of an inner desire to, and the knowledge that it is achievable. It is this kind of motivation that encourages us to do things purely out of interest and enjoyment.

There is an immense amount of research out there on motivational theories. If it is something you would like to find out more about, try searching on the internet for more information or reading a book such as *The Handbook of Communication Skills* edited by Owen Hargie (Routledge, 2006).

Why are goals important for young learners?

Goals help us to feel that we are on a learning *journey*; they help us to see that if we take certain steps we can achieve certain results. They are part of the process of breaking larger tasks down into manageable chunks and that is crucial for learning. After all, we'd never attempt anything if every task seemed so huge and unwieldy we can't find a way in.

Research has also shown us the following features of working towards goals:

- Those who work towards specific goals often perform better and achieve greater outcomes than those who are plodding along without any specific goals.
- The harder the goal gets (to a certain point), the better the performance of the person striving to reach the goal.
- Vague goals are not as effective in drawing out results as specific goals are. In other words, instead of saying 'give it a go', try something like 'answer the first part of that question and I'll come back and see how you're doing in two minutes'.

It's important to appreciate that there is a balance to be had. Too much pressure and the learner will lose interest in the goal and motivation will collapse. Too little and insufficient learning takes place and opportunities for growth and development are lost. You will learn just how much pressure you can apply to each child at any time, but as a rule of thumb, most can take just that little bit more stretching (within the realms of emotional safety) than you think! Don't necessarily stop when the goal has been reached. Take it onwards if time and motivation permits. One thing to be aware of though – just like adults, children's motivation to reach goals is subject to fluctuation. All kinds of things can affect it, from the weather to how much sleep they have had, from what they have eaten to how well they are getting on with their mates. Part of your task is to assess how significant these factors are for a child and work with that information. Flexibility, but with the aim of achieving, is the key.

Is it ever better not to set goals when trying to motivate some pupils?

Generally, it will usually be better to use goal setting when working with pupils. That said, you may sometimes need to play around with the ways in which goals are determined. Research has told us that goals are typically determined in three main ways:

- they can be *assigned* by others (or rather, 'imposed' by parents, teachers, bosses and so on)
- they can be *self-set*
- they can be *participative* (in other words, agreed through discussion).

There is no innately correct way of determining goals. Sometimes each method will be appropriate in the classroom. It goes without saying that you should discuss goal setting with the teacher before engaging in it with pupils, but don't feel that all goals should be self-set or participative. It's perfectly acceptable at times to assign a goal to a pupil. Self-setting is great when pupils are able to assess what they can realistically achieve in a given timeframe – having the tendency to over- or under-estimate this usually means that goal setting needs to be at least participative, if not assigned. Too much pressure, especially when self-imposed, can be as damaging as too little!

What is the best way of giving feedback to a pupil?

It is always a good idea to discuss this with the teacher you are working with as he/she may have devised a method for delivering feedback to pupils and consistency will be important. Your school as a whole may also have a policy on this. If, following the relevant discussions, it's clear that you will be expected to offer feedback to pupils in your own way, these guidelines will help:

- Remember that feedback is only of any value to the person receiving it if it is constructive. Sometimes, that's easier said than done! We're all human and responding spontaneously to certain types of behaviour or attitude is natural. In addition, it can sometimes be urgent to change a child's behaviour if they are about to cause harm to themselves or to others. Keep it constructive though, however sharply you have to respond.

- Research has shown that people are more likely to accept suggestions for change if they are presented as part of a feedback 'sandwich'. For example, offer a positive response, then a suggestion for improvement, and finally finish with another positive comment. So, when feeding back on behaviour, for example, you might say something along the lines of: 'You listened really well when Mrs Waters was speaking. Next time try to wait until she has finished before opening your work book. But I loved to see you so keen to get on with your work.' Another way of doing this that has become popular in many schools is to give 'two stars and a wish'; in other words, two areas of strength in the work a child has completed and one area for future development. Depending on the age of the children you work with this may be a useful strategy to adopt particularly as both the 'feedback sandwich' and 'two stars and a wish' work equally well when used verbally.

> It is important that TAs should be involved in the process of feeding back to pupils but only within the framework agreed between TA and teacher. Both need to be completely clear on where 'feedback' and 'assessment' begin and end.

Some children seem to need far more nurturing and motivation in their work than others do. Is it fair to treat them differently?

One of the aims of your work with children should be to encourage them to become independent and self-motivated learners. Some children will naturally be far further along that road than others so you will inevitably find yourself treating them differently. Remember, equality of opportunity does not necessarily mean treating all children in exactly the same way; it means treating each child in such a way as to ensure that they can reach their best potential. This typically means:

- boosting pupils' confidence as much as possible
- creating an atmosphere and environment that is conducive to safe and effective learning (even if you are working with a small group around a table, you can still ensure that the micro-environment you create is safe and positive)
- making sure that each task they do is set and paced to build on their learning (nothing too easy or too complex)
- ensuring that they can see the relevance in what they are doing.

If you are at all unsure about the way in which your time is divided between children when you are working in the classroom talk to the class teacher for advice. He/she will be able to tell you if you should be sharing your time differently.

How can I best recognise the efforts of each child?

You're right to acknowledge that each child needs to have his/her efforts recognised! The outcomes they produce may not all be the same, nor will the effort they put into them, but what they *do* achieve needs recognition.

While many schools have systems of reward such as stickers and merits, mentions in assembly or being included on the 'golden tree', and it is important for you to be consistent with these, never under-estimate the powerful strength of taking the time to say to a child: 'well done, I know how much you put into that and you have really done well, I'm very proud of you'. That kind of personal and focused interaction in their busy world is invaluable. If each child had this kind of attention on a regular basis they would soon learn to have respect for themselves and that is a tremendous gift for anyone!

What is the single most important thing to remember when motivating pupils?

There probably isn't one single factor, but it is worth keeping in mind that all humans like to feel that the people they are with enjoy spending time with them. If you can convey to the pupils you work with that it is a pleasure to be with them and not a chore or simply work for you, then you are bound to be able to develop more effective working relationships that motivate the pupils.

I sometimes wonder if teaching children time management skills might help them to stay motivated and on task. Would this be a good idea?

Learning about time management is generally a naturally 'caught' aspect of school life, but that said, some pupils will need substantial assistance organising their time so that they achieve what they need to and beyond. If you are working with pupils who struggle to complete a task through poor time management, try these ideas:

- Break each task down into manageable chunks.
- Keep them focused by giving each aspect of the task a time limit (for example, 'answer this question first and you have three minutes to do that').
- Let them know when half of the allocated time has passed. Remind them again when the time is nearly up. Then stop them working when the time has passed to review how much they have achieved. Did they realistically need more time? Did they manage that bite-sized workload well? Would they have benefited from the 'pressure' of less time?
- Think about ways in which you can mark time visually, perhaps with an egg timer, or audibly, with a quiet alarm of some kind.
- Encourage the pupils to be responsible for keeping a track of time too. Don't allow them to become too reliant on your input.

CHAPTER 6

All about behaviour

The job of an educator is to teach students to see the vitality in themselves.

(Joseph Campbell)

Introduction

Anyone who is remotely interested in the world of education in this country right now would be forgiven for thinking that the behaviour of young people has deteriorated. Media reports seem to be full with comments on their attitudes and antics, and the misdemeanours of the few obliterate the fact that the majority of young people are perfectly pleasant, decent members of our communities.

As a TA you will undoubtedly be involved in addressing pupils' behaviour during the course of your work in the classroom. Whether this be with specific pupils for whom challenging behaviour is already an identified issue, or more generally with groups of pupils who may require your input to keep them on track every now and then, your role in the classroom is key. Making this work most effectively takes constant collaboration with the class teacher, as well as your careful and timely interventions.

One of the most powerful tools that any adult can have when dealing with a child's behaviour that needs addressing is simply to acknowledge it. Just saying to a child who is tired, angry or aggressive that you know and can understand what is going on for them can help to diffuse a huge amount of tension. It helps to keep things calm and gives the child a voice that is heard, possibly for the first time. That act should never be under-estimated.

Far from being daunted by the prospect of dealing with poor behaviour, it is worth remembering that according to the Office for Standards in Education (Ofsted), the behaviour of pupils is absolutely no cause for concern in the majority of schools. Yes, some schools may have more than their fair share of behaviour difficulties to contend with but that is not most schools by any means.

This chapter focuses on the behaviour management of pupils and classroom life regarding behaviour in general.

FAQs in this chapter cover:

- Building working relationships with children
- Getting to know the children you work with
- Rewards and sanctions
- Understanding teachers' approaches to behaviour management
- Issues around listening
- Behaviour support plans (BSPs)/single education plans (SEPs)
- Noticing uncharacteristic behaviour patterns
- Contributing to behaviour management
- The physical restraint of pupils
- Relationships as a key to behaviour management
- Behaviour and equality issues
- Use of voice
- Developing assertiveness
- Dealing with emotional outbursts
- Collaborating with colleagues over behaviour management
- Winning over a difficult student

What is the single most important factor to remember when dealing with a child's misbehaviour?

As any good teacher will tell you, working with children is all about relationships. And managing their behaviour when it needs to be improved is reliant on the quality of the relationships you build with children in order to be successful. In addition, the relationships that you build up with the pupils you work with are subject to change. Many factors determine this, some of which are in your control (for example, the way in which you choose to respond to a child) and some are not (for example, the family row that took place in the child's home before he/she left for school). There are no magic solutions and some days will feel easier than others. Just as long as you are absolutely clear what the expectations of you are regarding behaviour management in the classroom you work in, you will be able to hold and handle most, if not all, situations you deal with. Working as a cohesive unit with the class teacher is essential.

It is also important to be aware of the fact that the way in which you work with pupils on their behaviour in the classroom will change over time, as you change and develop as a person and as a TA. You are utterly unique as a classroom practitioner and the best tools and techniques that you use will be those developed by you in response to the children you work with.

How important is it to get to know the children that you work with? Surely I'm there to help them with their school work?

You're employed in school to be a teaching assistant. Yes, that means that you are there to help children achieve the best they can but that in itself means developing working relationships with them that enable them to feel secure and understood in their school environment. Getting to know the children you work with is essential for that to happen and the more you can help them to feel that you are interested in them and that you want to know what life is like for them, the better. Naturally this does not need to dominate the time you spend working with them; you will need to guide them in achieving the work set by the teacher. But taking a keen interest in *their* interests will give you potentially endless paths to follow with them when learning is blocked or spirits are low.

In short, the children you teach are young people, with full lives, regardless of the nature of their backgrounds. The more you can encourage them to feel that you are interested in them as a *whole* person and not just a number in a busy classroom, the more likely you are to help bring out the best in them.

> If ever there is anything that you are uncertain of regarding behaviour management, always discuss this with the teacher(s) you work with or with the headteacher. It is so crucial that all adults working with children in your school are united in their expectations and tolerance levels. Make sure that you are fully part of the team in this respect.

When it comes to rewards and sanctions, can I devise my own methods for use in the classroom?

No, absolutely not. Unless, of course, you are told to by the teacher you are working with (which would be very unlikely). It is crucial that you follow the school's guidance closely when it comes to rewards and sanctions. There may well be a whole school policy on this, or it may be down to individual teachers to decide. Whatever the systems are that have been set up in your school, make sure that you know them and use them as instructed. If you are unsure about what your responsibilities are, always ask for clarification. This is such an important aspect of classroom life and can be carried out so differently from school to school. All the adults in the classroom have to be working with the same expectations regarding behaviour in order for the pupils to feel secure and safe, and to reduce the likelihood of the minority 'trying it on'.

If you have ideas on how behaviour might be tackled more effectively, perhaps regarding one particular child that you work with, then discuss these with the teacher(s) you work with. It is important to do this as you may have a slightly different perspective from that of the teacher because of the nature of your role in the classroom.

However, it remains the teacher's responsibility to determine the behaviour management policy of the classroom in accordance with the school's overall behaviour management policies.

The teacher I work with has told me I should feel free to use the sanctions that the school adopts for bad behaviour. I don't feel comfortable doing this. What should I do?

If you are ever in the position of not feeling comfortable about doing something that has been asked of you, always speak to the class teacher about it. The chances are once you have aired your concerns you will be able to reach a mutually agreeable arrangement.

Regarding the dishing out of sanctions, these pointers will help:

- Only ever do this in accordance with your school's behaviour management policy.
- If possible, check with the class teacher first before using a sanction – this won't always be possible but if it is, do so.
- Only ever use a sanction when you can explain calmly why it is being used; sanctions should never be given in anger or as a knee-jerk response to behaviour – don't fight fire with fire!
- Make sure the child (or children) know exactly *why* you have given the sanction – unless they understand, the sanction will only have a negative effect.
- Sanctions should never be used as a threat; promote the behaviour you want to see, rather than threaten what might happen should behaviour deteriorate.
- Never take back a reward as a sanction; this gives incredibly mixed messages.
- Always carry out any sanctions you use; once given you have to follow it through.
- Only ever use sanctions with the guilty; never a whole group or class.

The teacher that I work with doesn't always pick up on every incident in the classroom and it frustrates me sometimes. Is there anything that I can do?

Some teachers make a conscious decision not to 'fight every battle'. If they did, it could be exhausting and seriously eat into the time available for good quality teaching and learning. However, in some cases it may simply be that they are not aware of what is going on (and it would be unrealistic to expect one teacher to see everything), which is where having an extra pair of eyes in the classroom can be tremendously beneficial.

A good way to tackle this would be to make time to talk to the teacher about what your role might be. Ask him/her whether they would appreciate you stepping in to correct behaviour when it is possible to do this without disrupting the flow of a lesson, making sure that you know exactly how this should be achieved. Get ground rules like this sorted out sooner rather than later and you are more likely to be able to work as a cohesive unit bringing up the standards of behaviour in the classroom.

Do also make sure that you find out exactly what the teacher's approach to behaviour management is. Take time to gain this understanding and his/her methods may make more sense!

Should I expect pupils to listen to me as much as they listen to their teacher?

Yes! As far as the pupils are concerned you are equals and what you say should be adhered to just as much as what any other adult in the room says. It is important to add, too, that the general rule in the classroom should be that all people are listened to – pupils and adults alike – and that each has a time to talk and a time to listen.

If you feel that there is a difference in the way in which pupils treat you and the way in which they treat their teacher, make sure that you take time to discuss your concerns with the teacher you work with.

I've heard mention of BSPs for pupils with specific behavioural difficulties. What are these and are they something I would be involved in?

BSPs were statements that were actually prepared by the local authority detailing all the arrangements in the local areas for children with
behavioural difficulties. These plans were devised in consultation
with local headteachers, governors, school teaching and support
staff and so on. Their purpose was to aim to ensure that there are
'coherent, comprehensive and well understood local arrangements
for helping schools tackle poor behaviour and discipline problems'
(www.TeacherNet.co.uk). They detailed the support available to
schools and parents for handling behavioural problems and they
encouraged the sharing of good practice.

However, recent changes to the requirements for BSPs mean that
local authorities now have an SEP which covers a range of issues
including behaviour. The plan is designed to set out how local
authorities envisage raising standards and attainment, and what the
basis is for challenge and support in that process.

In answer to the question, no, this is not something that TAs
would be involved in directly, but it is something that they should
be aware of.

> You will find your local authority's SEP on its website. You may also
> want to talk to the teacher(s) you work with or your school's
> headteacher if you would like to find out more about the SEP in your
> area.

I understand that as a TA I am supposed to be aware of uncharacteristic behaviour patterns in the pupils I work with but what kinds of things should I be looking out for?

There is no set list, as this is the kind of thing that becomes far easier
to do with experience and as you get to know the pupils you work

with. Each child is different and will express themselves in their own unique way. That said, subtle changes in behaviour can indicate underlying causes beyond the usual ups and downs of growing up: causes such as bullying, substance abuse, child abuse and so on. As a TA who knows a child well, you are in a good position to detect growing extroversion or introversion, moodiness and belligerence, disinterest in work, disruption, an inability to maintain friendships and so on, and to pass the information on to the relevant person in school.

I didn't expect behaviour management to be an issue in primary school, especially in the younger classes, but it does seem to be sometimes. How can I contribute to managing behaviour in the classroom as a TA?

There are seemingly endless behaviour management strategies out there and some schools adopt whole school approaches, which every staff member abides by. Usually, however, a school has a behaviour management policy and although all staff will follow this policy (or at least, they should), there is usually room for individual teachers to create their own model for behaviour management in their classroom. For this reason it is really important to discuss with the teacher you are working with exactly what their expectations are regarding your input with behaviour management.

In general terms, when helping a child to transform his/her behaviour, either in the present moment (for example, stopping a child from causing another harm) or in the longer term (remember, sometimes it's an ongoing process), you need to work on developing great communication between you and the child. In particular, the child needs to feel listened to, even if you then have to address what is being said. Have crystal clear expectations of the child, building trust between you (a little give and take can help with this) and addressing all behaviour issues by demonstrating emotional intelligence. This way, behaviour can be addressed with the minimum of fuss and learning can resume as speedily as possible; and that is always the aim. Above all else, don't fight every battle. It simply isn't necessary and is invariably counter-productive.

> If in any doubt at all about behaviour management in the classroom, talk to the teacher(s) you are working with. The class has to know that all the adults in the classroom are working together to the same expectations and standards. If they spot differences, they may try, however subconsciously, to 'divide and conquer'. For their levels of security and safety in learning, you need to be as consistent as possible.

As a TA would I ever be expected to physically restrain a child?

You should be told exactly what the policy in your school is for the physical restraint of children. At the time of writing, it is proposed to extend the right that teachers have to restrain a child under certain circumstance to TAs. This is never something that schools undertake lightly and if you are in any doubt at all about if and how this should be done, make sure you speak to the headteacher as soon as possible.

> Your union will be able to tell you all you need to know about this issue. Make sure you know precisely what the circumstances are under which children can be restrained and how this can be done safely.

Is it true that behaviour management is all about the relationships between pupils and the adults working with them?

There are many different behaviour management systems and models out there and your school may well adopt one of them, or it may simply have created its own policy for behaviour management. But what lies at the heart of the effective management of behaviour in the classroom is the relationship that the adults in the room have with the pupils as individuals and as a whole class. Behaviour may seem like one of the most complex aspects of school life, but what it boils down to is pretty simple. Work on developing effective relationships that are strong enough in mutual respect to withstand the times when you need to reprimand and the times when the child is angry and frustrated with you, and you are well on the way to managing just about any type of behaviour a child can throw at you.

I've noticed that the teacher I work with doesn't treat all pupils the same when it comes to behaviour management. Is this right?

It's important to ask the teacher you work with about any aspect of their classroom practice that you cannot fully understand. It could well be appropriate to have different expectations of pupils regarding behaviour, especially if some have had particular difficulties in the past. Sometimes, behaviour management isn't so much about getting all children to behave in the same way as it is about getting the best behaviour out of each child. Often, the two approaches are significantly different.

I find I have to raise my voice sometimes when I'm working with certain children. Is this acceptable? Teachers often do, but they are dealing with a whole class.

It is not ideal to raise your voice to a child unless you need to attract their attention to protect them from imminent harm. If you are simply trying to alter their behaviour, there are other techniques far more effective than shouting, which is disruptive and potentially harmful to your voice among other things.

Instead of shouting, or even raising your voice when seeking to address a child's behaviour, try these ideas:

- Reinforce what you want them to be doing, not what you don't want them to be doing; praise the good, more than you focus on the negative.
- Keep your praise for a child crystal clear; do not give mixed messages.
- Make sure that they know exactly how they should be behaving rather than telling them what not to do.
- Make sure you employ a range of signals that pupils are doing the right thing, from a simple smile or thumbs up to verbal praise and feedback to adopting any of the rewards policy as discussed with the teacher(s) you work with.
- Most of the children you work with will be fluent in at least two languages — body and English! Be aware of what your body language is saying just as much as being aware of the words you use and your tone of delivery.

> It is worth making the effort to remember how certain techniques are received by individual pupils. You'll soon learn what makes each of them grow in self-respect and that has to be the aim of any attempt to correct or transform behaviour. Flexibility is key.

I don't always feel very assertive when I'm in the classroom. Is there anything I can do about that?

It's natural to experience fluctuations in your feelings of assertiveness. We're all human and none of us feels consistently assertive all the time. That said, assertiveness is an essential classroom skill and sometimes when we don't *feel* it, we have to *act as if* we do. Without assertiveness, our self-confidence and self-respect come into question and we are more likely to come over as being closed to the views of others.

There are many ways in which we can develop our assertiveness when necessary. Joining an evening class or reading one of the many books available on the issue can help, as may these ideas:

- What you say and the way in which you say it need to be consistent with one another. Your body language and the words you use should both demonstrate your assertiveness. Make sure that the language you use is direct (leave no room for ambiguity) and address the situation or behaviour, not the person. Never get personal.

- Keep your body language open and friendly, not closed and hostile or defensive.

- Keep your language simple and state clearly what it is you want from the situation.

- Use 'I' statements – 'I would like you to concentrate on this please'.

- Never be afraid to be assertive. It won't make you less popular; much the opposite in fact!

I have no idea what I would do if a child I was working with got really angry. What is the best way to deal with this?

First of all it's important to acknowledge that this is very rare. And if it does happen, there should be systems set up in your school to manage it, which should be explained to you when you start work. As a TA, you may be working with a small group alone (or at least, with the teacher being busy elsewhere), but you should always be within easy reach of support. If you are not sure where that support would come from in your school in such an event, make sure you find out as soon as possible. Knowing who to call on and when to ask for intervention from another adult can make all the difference in containing a situation and preventing it from escalating.

Witnessing strong emotions in someone can be difficult to handle, particularly so when that person is young and not fully aware of, or in control of, what they are feeling. These steps should help if ever you find yourself faced with an excessively angry child:

- The safety of the child and his/her classmates as well as you and any other adults in the room must come first. If you think that the child may cause harm to himself or to others send for assistance immediately (you would do this by asking another child to get someone – be specific – rather than by leaving the situation yourself).

- Don't get angry yourself. Stay calm and say calming things. Tell the child that everything is OK. Don't respond specifically to what he/she is saying at that moment. Keep quiet and controlled. The idea is to present an example – you're displaying the kind of behaviour you want the child to mimic.

- Offer the child somewhere to go outside the classroom and away from his/her source of anger. If this is refused, keep offering at regular intervals.

- Make sure that the child has the opportunity to 'get it all out', but this should happen away from other children in a safe environment, preferably with someone who is experienced in dealing with emotional outbursts (the headteacher, a counsellor, or behaviour support worker or similar).

- Don't make demands of the child. Issue clear unambiguous instructions rather than hollering orders. Your body language, tone and volume should be calm and give the child space to respond to what you say, however they choose to do that. Even if they have 'lost it', you can still be an example of how they need to communicate.

- *Always* follow up on incidents such as strong emotional outbursts. Even if this means passing the information on to the teacher to follow up. There will be reasons for this temporary loss of control in the child and these need to be determined as soon as possible. Make a written record of exactly what happened, what led to it, what was said, what you did to try to calm the situation and what the outcome was. Pass these notes on to the teacher and/or headteacher.

Do keep in mind that if you should witness an emotional outburst by a child it would be incredibly rare for you to be the cause. You would be seeing the outcome of a build up of tension in the child that may have been taking place for days (or hours at least). Don't blame yourself, but do talk to a trusted colleague or friend if the incident has left you feeling shaken up.

Should TAs share information about the behaviour of children they work with or is it better to approach each child without the impressions and opinions of others ringing in your mind?

It's right to take the attitude that each child will behave differently with each adult he/she works with. Behaviour is all about relationships and the dynamics between two people are never repeated. That said, some degree of sharing of information can be incredibly useful and the more these kinds of professional conversations go on in schools the better it is for the children.

For any information about a child you receive in this way think to yourself, how does this help me to work better with him/her in the classroom? If you can't apply it for this purpose, you probably don't need to know it. Above all else, the school's guidance on confidentiality in the classroom should be adhered to.

If you are job sharing classroom support for a particular child with another TA it would be advisable to communicate regularly (either in person or through a communications book), but again, be aware that no child will work in an identical way with two different adults. This kind of shared information can inform your work with a child but should not direct or dictate it.

There is one particular child who I find very hard to get on with. I know I should be able to get over this but how?

This is perfectly natural and most, if not all, teachers and TAs will have experienced this at some stage. But it is worth keeping in mind that there is always something that can be done to improve your relationships with children, particularly those you find difficult to get on with.

Personality clashes are impossible to eradicate – we are all different and it would be crazy to suggest that we can get on equally well with everyone. But there are ways of improving your relationships with pupils and of focusing on the positive strands of your time spent working together. These ideas may help:

- Remember to always focus on the behaviour and not on the child. Each child you work with is so much more than the behaviour they display so never ever let any conversations deteriorate into the personal. You can alter behaviour; personalities are far harder to influence! This approach also makes it easier to find something that you like about the child too.
- Even though you may be struggling with your feelings about a particular child, always continue niceties such as greeting them by name and with a smile. Take opportunities to speak to them when you see them around the school; anything to help break down barriers.
- Have the expectation that he/she will cooperate with you.
- Create opportunities for this child to succeed and feel good in your company.
- Depending on the age of the child, you could aim to work at coming to a mutual understanding about what is wrong and how it might be fixed. Always give the child an opportunity to respond with their 'side' of the situation. This is suitable for older, more mature children.

- Focus on what *does* work with the child and replicate this as much as possible in your time working together. Aim to identify the circumstances under which this child is most cooperative.
- Hook into the child's genuine interests. Aim to find some common ground and build on it. Is there something that you both love? Sport for example, or a particular food?
- Aim to build the child's self-respect. This will help to reduce the chances of him/her being uncooperative and will help to encourage resilience and resourcefulness.
- Positively reinforce any unique aspects of his/her work or contribution to school life.
- Make sure that the child's attitude does not emerge from frustration. Can he/she access the learning? Are there any simple adjustments that can be made so that he/she can read the board and hear instructions clearly? Be aware of over- and under-stimulation.
- Always give crystal clear instructions broken down into basic stages if necessary.
- Talk to the teacher(s) you work with about addressing any unmet emotional needs that could be impacting the child's behaviour, perhaps through circle time or other discussion periods in class.

It's important not to spend so much time focusing on how this particular child ticks that other responsibilities on your plate get neglected. It is always worth working to create better relationships but do keep it all in perspective.

You never have to tackle behaviour and relationship issues alone in a school. There is always someone else who can help you out, whether that is the class teacher, the headteacher, the SENCO or another member of the support staff. Yes, personalities do play an important role in all relationships, but you will always be able to pick up tips and tricks from others should you need to.

CHAPTER 7

Personal issues

> Set me a task in which I can put something of myself, and it is a
> task no longer; it is a joy; it is an art.
>
> (Bliss Carmen)

Introduction

So, you're working in a school, fully immersed into the nitty-gritty of
day-to-day life there and the chances are you are enjoying every
minute. The children you work with are great fun and the teachers
truly appreciate what you do for them. There may be the occasional
drama that tests your endurance and tenacity, or the odd temporary
blip that leads to anxiety or stress, but on the whole, all is well.

Yet there may still be times when personal issues edge into your
working life, causing disruption, or when you need your work to
offer you the kind of flexibility that you routinely offer to it.
When this happens it is important to remember that no one is
only their job role. We all carry out multiple roles in addition to
what we get paid for and holding on to an holistic view of our life
invariably helps us to be more effective at what it is that gives us
money.

This chapter explores the kind of personal issues that might
arise that impact TAs at work and the ways in which they can be
handled.

FAQs in this chapter cover:

- Catching frequent infections
- Taking time off through illness
- Being a school governor
- Over-bonding with children
- Changing jobs
- Support groups for TAs
- Non-sick leave during the school term
- Time off to look after sick children
- Time off for moving house
- Financial help for buying a home
- Understanding payslips
- Beating self-criticism

Since starting work as a TA I seem to be catching frequent infections. These are never enough for me to take time off but they make me feel below par and lacking in energy. I know I could do my job better if I didn't catch them. What can I do?

You will soon hit the point of exhaustion if you don't address the emotional and physical demands on you so it is good to address how you are feeling. Frequent infections could be down to the fact that you are working in a school with millions of bugs constantly attacking your immune system. They could also be down to an underlying health condition that requires attention and for that reason it is important to seek the advice of your chosen health care provider. Talk through your symptoms and how you are feeling emotionally with him/her. It may be that you could benefit from taking some time off or reducing your workload temporarily, or it could be that you just need to boost your immunity and perhaps take up some form of exercise.

The important thing is to seek professional advice. Don't plod on indefinitely feeling permanently under the weather. Take opportunities to nurture yourself by eating healthily and taking early nights, and seek and accept support for a while. Taking these kinds of small steps can bring about big changes in the way in which you feel.

I sometimes turn up at school when I should really have taken a day off but I don't want to let the teacher down. She seems to rely on me being there and has often said that she doesn't know what she would do without me there. Should I feel obliged to turn up no matter what?

It doesn't matter how reliant a teacher is on you as their TA, it's unlikely they will want you to turn up coughing and spluttering when a day off would be more beneficial! OK, you do have an obligation to turn up for work unless you are truly ill, but if you should really be spending the day in bed then you are unlikely to be much use to anyone if you are at work.

It's great to be relied upon and this shows that your working relationship is healthy; healthy enough to take the hit of you not being there when you are not fit to be. In addition, not allowing your body to repair itself when it is unwell undoubtedly leads to greater health issues further down the road. It's simply not worth that gamble.

If at all possible, give the teacher(s) notice of when you will not be at school, but don't worry if this doesn't happen. Beyond that, just concentrate on getting fit and back into the classroom as soon as possible.

Is it true that I could become a school governor as a TA? If so, how can I find out more about it?

Yes, TAs can become school governors and are usually welcomed on governing bodies. There are many positive advantages that TAs can bring to governing bodies, not least their unique perspective on life in the school and the learning that takes place. They have a real insight into the children they support, especially those with SEN, and their expertise can really be invaluable to governors when they are thinking about the policies and needs for the school. In addition, support staff can provide a sometimes well-needed reality check! They know what life is really like in the school from all kinds of perspectives and governing bodies that have TAs on them appreciate that kind of input.

I feel that I am over-bonding with a particular child. I know that I give her more attention than I give to others and I feel very sorry for her and what life has given her so far. I know that I should remain professional about this but I don't know how to handle it. What should I do?

You're human! This happens! But you're absolutely right to recognise what is going on and seek to address it. The worst thing for the child would be to build up a reliance on you and your sympathy for her. Your ideal role is to provide appropriate support for her while she is at school and in your care and an important aspect of that is for her to see that you treat others with equal care and attention.

If the child is becoming 'clingy' you could talk to the teacher about how the two of you might distract her attention and focus her elsewhere. This doesn't mean that you start to ignore her but it does mean that you share your attentions more equally and allow her the space to grow with independence.

There is no reason why you cannot continue to support her as you would any other child, but she will move on out of the class and through her life and the best gift you can give her is your calm, consistent and appropriate interest in her well-being.

> If this situation is causing you difficulties, talk to a trusted colleague or friend. It is only natural to develop an interest in what is going on for the children you work with but it is crucial, for their emotional well-being, that you keep it all in balance.

I am not enjoying my job at all and think that it is time for me to leave and move on. How do I go about this and what period of notice would I have to give?

It's great to recognise when your job satisfaction is not what it might be. This is far better than plodding on in an environment that doesn't suit you for the sake of a job that you are not enjoying. Before writing a letter of resignation, take a few moments to consider whether there is anything that can be done in your current situation to improve your job satisfaction. Consider the following points:

- Can the working relationship between you and the teacher be improved upon in any way?
- Would you prefer to be working with a different year group or age phase?
- Do you feel supported in your work?
- Are you happy in the wider environment of the school? Or do you feel that you don't fit in?

You may want to consider discussing how you feel with the head-teacher and teacher(s) you work with to see if there is anything that can be done to reinvigorate your enthusiasm for the job. Sometimes that is all that is needed to realise that it is not *all* aspects of a job that are getting you down, but just *some*.

If, however, you remain sure that the job is not for you, it would be appropriate for you to move on to new pastures for the sake of your own sanity and the greater good of the school and its pupils. In order to leave, you will need to write a letter of resignation to the headteacher. This simply needs to state the facts although most heads will be interested in why you are moving on. It is well worth doing this as amicably as possible, regardless of the circumstances of your decision to leave. You never know whether you'll be asking him/her to write a reference for you in the future!

Regarding notice periods, these will be set out in your contract. If you are at all unsure about how much notice you must give, talk to your headteacher about it.

It is usually, although not always, easier to gain new employment if you are already in a post. You may want to consider this if you are thinking about leaving with nothing lined up to go to.

Finally, take your decision to move on to be a positive thing. Who knows what the future may now hold for you!

Are there any local support groups for TAs? I sometimes feel it would be good to be able to talk to other TAs from outside my school just to get an idea of how things work in their school. It would be useful to share ideas and information.

Some local authorities have TA networks so that TAs from different schools can meet and discuss work issues or share ideas and behaviour approaches. You could ask your headteacher to see if any such network exists in your authority. Check out the authority's website too as details may be posted on there. If nothing exists, why not start something up? Talk to other TAs in your school to see what support there would be for the idea before approaching your local authority about organising something.

What happens if I need to have some time off school during the hours when I would normally be working? Is there any room for negotiation?

This depends entirely on the school. Some schools are very open to accommodating TAs' requests for time off for events such as their children's participation in a school play or to attend a graduation ceremony or wedding for example. However, other schools take a hard line on requests for time off during working hours. You would really need to find out what your school's policy is.

Never feel that you can't ask your headteacher about this, but once you know exactly how your school operates regarding this kind of leave, don't push it by asking twice if the response was negative. Working in a school is a wonderful experience, but it does have its limitations in that term dates are set and there is very little flexibility for staff. It is generally expected that all employees respect and understand this when accepting a job in a school, although many heads will appreciate that the world doesn't necessarily fit in around term dates! At best, you may be granted unpaid leave or the opportunity to make time up at a later date if you need time off during term time. At worst, the answer will be 'no'.

If my own children are ill am I entitled to take time off to look after them?

This is a difficult area for schools and working parents to negotiate but within reason there may be occasions when you have no choice but to stay at home to look after a sick child. However, you are contracted to work certain hours at particular times and if you require too much flexibility on your contract, the school is likely to start asking questions.

If you have no choice but to take time off to look after a sick child, be open about this as soon as possible. The head is likely to be sympathetic, as long as it happens only very rarely. If you can foresee a time when you may need a sustained amount of time off, discuss the possibility of compassionate leave with the headteacher.

Never feel that you can't discuss these kinds of issues with your school. Life happens, and there are times for everyone when the balance between work responsibilities and home responsibilities gets out of kilter. The worst thing you can do is put your head in the sand and hope it all works out. Inform your head sooner rather than later and be open to creative solutions to the problem.

I understand that school staff are entitled to time off for moving house. Is this really the case?

Any time off that is not for sickness or maternity purposes is purely down to the governing body of a school to decide. Many schools do recognise that major events such as moving house can't always be timed for the holidays or weekends and will grant a day or two for these purposes but this will almost always be unpaid leave. There are no set rules though so if you need to take time off for this purpose talk to your headteacher about it as early as possible. He/she will be able to tell you if you need to approach the governing body by letter or if that decision-making role has been delegated to the head. For one day's leave it is likely that the head will be able to give you a decision.

If you do not want to go for the unpaid option you could ask your headteacher if you can make up the hours at another time. This may be a possibility.

I have heard that there is a key worker scheme for teachers to help them to buy a house. Does this apply to TAs too? I would love to buy somewhere to live in the community I am working in but the current house price crisis is making it impossible.

There are key worker schemes to make it easier for certain workers to get a foot on the property 'ladder' but these typically do not include TAs. Other programmes sometimes run by local authorities or private providers may offer non-key workers (which is ironically how TAs are usually classed) assistance for home purchasing but there is no single national arrangement for this. These programmes are dependent on occupation and local need along with other criteria.

It is essential that you find out exactly what the consequences are of purchasing a home through an affordable housing scheme. There will be terms and conditions that you should be aware of and you should be perfectly clear about what percentage of the property you would eventually own and how vulnerable you might be to rising rents (on the part of the property you are not purchasing) or fluctuating interest rates. These schemes are not suitable for everyone and it is important that you do your homework on them.

There are many people who believe that the current housing bubble is about to, or already has, burst causing a long-term downward adjustment in house prices ('crashes' never happen overnight – they typically take several years to unfold). These people urge against over-stretching financially in order to buy a home in the current climate. House prices are historically cyclical. What goes up can come down. You can find out more from websites such as www.global housepricecrash.co.uk and www.pricedout.org.uk. Always do your own research when considering making a major purchase like a home. Never be taken in by those who encourage you strongly one way or another; the chances are they have a vested interest in convincing you to do what they say or are basing their advice on outdated information!

The Department for Communities and Local Government website has all the information and contacts you need on appointed housing associations that offer 'affordable housing options'. Note that each region operates a different system according to local need. Visit www.communities.gov.uk or telephone 020 7944 4400 8.30 a.m.–5.30 p.m. Monday–Friday for further information.

I don't understand my payslip. It seems overly complicated and I'm not sure about the deductions that have been made. Where can I find out more about this?

Some payslips do seem to have been designed to test even the most numerate among us so don't worry about not fully understanding exactly what all the entries on them mean. You're certainly not alone! You can find out more about what each aspect of the payslip refers to from several sources. Try these:

- your school's bursar
- the headteacher
- your local authority's payroll department.

Make sure that you do understand any explanations you are given. It is not unheard of for mistakes to be made with salaries, for example, regarding tax codes, so if anything is wrong, or entered in error, it should be corrected as soon as possible and any owed back pay would usually be included in the next month's salary.

I sometimes find that I am very self-critical at work, always telling myself that I could do more. How can I gain a better perspective?

This is just your inner critic running on overdrive! We all have one and at times it just needs to take a break or we'll end up feeling inadequate and demoralised. Some self-talk is essential, it provides us with feedback and ideas, but the kind of persistent negativity you describe is not helpful. Try these ideas for perspective:

- As soon as you recognise that your inner critic has kicked in, think about three positive features of yourself and your work. The aim is to counteract your self-criticisms with self-acknowledgement.
- Aim to discover the circumstances in which your inner critic gets going. What winds it up? Is it when you are feeling low about other aspects of your life and those feelings of frustration are being directed towards your work? Or is it when you could genuinely improve your work performance? Aim to gain a greater understanding of the root of this kind of self-talk.
- Be aware of when your inner critic is calm and supportive and when it is actively criticising.
- What tames your inner critic? Gain self-awareness and self-observance and you'll be able to use this kind of critical feedback for positive benefit.

CHAPTER 8

Working with colleagues and parents

Individual commitment to a group effort – that is what makes a team work, a company work, a society work, a civilization work.
(Vince Lombardi)

Introduction

The key to working effectively as a TA is developing great relationships with those you work with. Naturally this cannot be simply down to you! Relationships take at least two to be effective and communication will be key.

If you have been a TA for a number of years you will know that the dynamics between you and the teacher depend on the personalities involved and the degree of mutual respect and trust between you. Likewise, the relationships you develop with the parents of the children you work with are not simply down to you. The need for commitment to make these connections work for the best outcome possible for the children rests with all involved.

This chapter explores some of the ways in which TAs can work with teachers, other colleagues and parents in order to ensure that the pupils are served best.

FAQs in this chapter cover:

- Teachers and TAs as partners
- Hierarchies in the classroom
- Staying in touch with fellow TAs
- Building strong working relationships
- Choosing who you work with
- Workplace bullying
- Communicating with parents
- Confidentiality issues
- Clashes with parents
- Working with governors
- Being included in school functions
- Socialising outside school
- Reviewing working relationships
- Using report sheets
- Meeting with SENCOs
- Bilingual TAs

Are teachers and TAs partners in the classroom?

Yes, ideally they should be, with the TA working under the direction of the teacher, fully informed about the teacher's plans and intentions for the teaching and learning that takes place.

Is it helpful for TAs to think of themselves as the junior partner in the relationship between TA and teacher?

No, it's not helpful and it's not necessarily true. There is a natural hierarchy in the classroom in that the teacher is the senior leader in the room, but in terms of the tasks you must perform, you should acknowledge that your contribution is unique and valuable. Teachers and TAs have different roles in schools so direct comparisons are not helpful. You are a team and within that team, you would usually defer to the teacher's judgement on any arising issues. That said, the dynamics between you and the teacher may be such that there are certain areas in which the teacher would defer to *your* judgement, depending on your skills and expertise. It's all about building a working relationship that is respectful of the skills and talents of both people, and recognising that this will mature over time.

Should TAs working in one school have the chance to meet each other on a regular basis?

Ideally, yes. It can be incredibly useful for TAs to communicate with other TAs, not least because this helps to guard against feelings of isolation arising. Regular meetings in school for TAs to attend are a good idea, as are opportunities for TAs to meet with the SENCO, their line manager or the member of the senior leadership team with responsibilities for TAs. These needn't be frequent – perhaps just once every half term – but schools that do operate such a system report that these meetings are an excellent way of making sure that TAs are kept up to date not only with the developments in the school, but also with the work of other TAs.

> If such meetings are not formally arranged at your school, don't under-estimate the value of getting something up and running yourself. Talk to your headteacher about the idea. He/she may be able to find out from the local authority the best way of linking up with other TAs.

I am having difficulty building a good working relationship with the teacher I work with most closely. Is there anything I can do to help this?

The most important thing you can do initially is to communicate. Most relationship issues stem from insufficient communication and the sooner you can both address this the better. It is also important to look at the way in which you are currently working. Have an open and honest discussion about the limitations of your contract and working hours and the fact that you both have to work within that framework. This may well be the source of some of the frustration that is felt. It is also worth exploring exactly what the teacher feels about having you in their room. If they feel watched or judged in any way (regardless of whether you actually *are* judging them — although you are not there to judge — it's how they *feel* that matters) they may well resent your presence in the room. Do also take time to determine exactly what you think may be the cause of the friction and be prepared to discuss this rationally and openly with a view to reaching a mutually agreeable solution.

If you feel that there is a genuine personality clash between you and the teacher you should speak to the head as soon as possible. It may be that the head organises a mediated meeting between you both so that your differences can be expressed in a safe space. If an understanding cannot be reached so that you can work effectively together, you may be redeployed elsewhere in the school. This would, however, be an extreme step and most heads will want all parties involved to resolve the issue rather than be defeated by it.

Will I ever get the chance to choose which teacher I work with?

Some larger schools offer teachers and TAs the chance to express a preference for who they would like to work with in the new academic year. Most schools, however, do not have this level of flexibility and staff generally work where they are told to. There should not be a reason for this to be a problem — as a TA you should be happy to work with any staff member — but if there is a genuine reason why you would not be able to work productively with a particular person make sure that you speak to the headteacher as soon as possible.

I feel quite intimidated by one particular colleague. Someone suggested that they may actually be bullying me. Is there anything that I can do about it?

Bullying in the workplace can and does go on and it can be hard to recognise at first especially when it is unexpected. If you think that you may be experiencing bullying at work, these steps will help:

• Talk to a trusted friend or colleague about what is happening. Their perspective will help you to form an opinion about what might be going on.
• Talk to the headteacher about what is happening. Again, do this from the angle of gaining a fresh perspective (although do not allow yourself to be convinced that nothing is going on if you feel it is).
• Re-read your job description so that you remind yourself of exactly what you are supposed to be doing at work.
• Read up on assertiveness.
• Contact your union for advice on dealing with bullying in the workplace.
• Keep a written record of all communication between you and this colleague.
• Refute all unfair claims made about you and/or your work.
• Monitor changes in your work performance that you think may have been caused by the treatment you are receiving from this person.

You do not have to put up with bullying or intimidating behaviour and have the right to expect full support from the headteacher or other members of the senior leadership team to resolve the issue amicably. If you think that your health may be suffering as a result of this situation at work, talk to your chosen health care provider (for example, your GP). Don't struggle on alone without seeking help. Workplace bullying is illegal on several grounds and once your head is made aware of the situation you are dealing with he/she should ensure that all is resolved as soon as possible.

> You can find out more about workplace bullying from www.bullyonline.org.

As a TA do I have any need to communicate with parents? Surely that is the teacher's job?

Technically yes, it is part of the teacher's role to communicate with parents, but there will undoubtedly be times when it is appropriate for you to communicate with parents too. This can be the case particularly if a parent has difficulty, for whatever reason, in discussing an issue with the teacher. In such situations, the TA can be a helpful intermediary.

It is important to remember that any communication with parents should be reported back to the teacher, preferably in writing, although this may not always be practical. You may have your own arrangements on how such communication should be followed up but do be aware that everything should be conveyed to the teacher. It would be inappropriate for you to discuss anything with a parent 'in confidence' as the chances are you would need to pass important information on to another member of staff at the school. If any parent asks to speak to you in confidence, refer them to the teacher or headteacher.

If a parent wants to make a complaint about the school and sees you as being the person to make it to, politely remind them of the school's complaints procedure and report back to the teacher the details of the conversation. It is not your responsibility to act as a messenger for parents.

If you are working closely with a child with SEN you will almost certainly need to communicate with his/her parents to help ensure consistency of approach between the programme provided for the child at school and the support the parents give at home. It will become clear when working in your school how best to achieve this kind of communication. There may even be formal structures set up to facilitate that or it may happen on an ad hoc basis.

> If ever you are in doubt about whether you should be speaking to a parent direct, talk to the class teacher. Don't ever feel you have to enter into a discussion with a parent simply because you have been collared in the playground. It is perfectly acceptable for anything beyond basic greetings to be referred to the teacher or head by TAs.

My friend's son is really playing up at school. Should I tell her?

This is a very difficult situation to navigate but the answer is that you should not say anything. The child is entitled to expect you to treat what happens in the classroom in confidence. If there is genuine cause for talking to his parents about his behaviour, the teacher will do this through the proper procedure in your school. If you step in without discussing your concerns with the teacher you may end up doing more harm than good. If you are worried about your friend's son and his progress at school, discuss the issue with the teacher and not your friend.

> Confidentiality in the classroom is an important dimension of the work of a TA. This does not mean keeping concerns to yourself. It means raising concerns through the appropriate channels sooner rather than later.

What would I do if a parent asked me questions about their child in the playground?

Beyond saying a few words about the child's progress ('Billy did really well today') the playground is not really the place to get into discussions about a child. Parents at the school will know exactly what process to go through if they have any concerns they want to raise and collaring staff in the playground is not part of it!

The best way to deal with this is to politely ask if they would like to make an appointment with the class teacher. If the teacher is available then and there you could find out if it is possible to arrange a meeting but otherwise it would be appropriate to ask the parent to ring the school to make an appointment. This isn't about being unavailable to parents, but rather it is about ensuring that issues are dealt with in the most effective way possible. Playground discussions are rarely effective, but a pre-arranged meeting where each participant has had the opportunity to consider in advance the issue in hand is.

In addition, some headteachers make themselves available at going home time should any issues arise so if you feel cornered and a senior member of staff is in sight, don't hesitate to call on them.

Above all else, never feel compelled to get into a discussion about a child when you have not had the opportunity to discuss the situation with the child's teacher. You do not have to deal with these kinds of situations alone.

There are issues of confidentiality to be aware of when discussing children and what goes on in the classroom(s) you work in. Never be drawn if you feel that you will be crossing a confidentiality line. Always seek the advice of the teacher or headteacher if you are feeling pressured by a parent.

One particular parent is making my life a misery. She constantly criticises the work I do with her child and it's making me lose interest. What can I do about it?

You're right to want to resolve this issue before your work with the child is affected. It is not the child's fault but a 'pushy' parent can do more harm than good if they do not approach a school through the correct channels.

If a parent seeks to undermine your work, don't dismiss their views out of hand. It could be that there are some improvements that might be made and parents' views are always to be considered. However, you do not need to do this in such a way that makes you feel put down or unduly criticised. Don't take this kind of situation personally. Talk to the teacher about your feelings and ask that he/she arrange to meet the parent concerned. Ideally you should be present at this meeting too. Calmly listen to what the parent has to say and if you feel that any comments are unfair or unreasonable, calmly say so and request that another meeting be arranged at which these issues of dispute can be discussed.

You do not have to deal with situations like this alone and should expect the full support of the teacher and headteacher. Do not let incidents like this affect your confidence in the classroom. Criticism can be great if it is constructive; it propels us towards making improvements and becoming more effective. Constant undermining, however, serves no purpose and should be quashed immediately. You do not have to tolerate it.

If you are left feeling that the matter has not been dealt with effectively through the meetings you have had with the parent, you may want to discuss the matter with your union for further advice.

Would I ever need to have anything to do with school governors?

That depends entirely on how active your school's governors are! In some schools the governors are very hands-on and are often seen in the classroom and helping out around the school. In other schools, they simply meet after school hours and are rarely seen when the real work of the school takes place.

Governors, when working to greatest effect, are a school's 'critical friends'. Therefore it is likely that you will come across governors at some stage. Whether they are visiting a classroom to find out more about the teaching and learning that is taking place or specifically exploring the work of TAs in the school, they should be present to some degree and actively interested in your work as a TA.

You should have been told when you started at the school (and when any changes occurred) who the staff governors are. There may be several on the school's governing body. Remember, staff governors are not there to represent staff in the way that a union representative represents members. It's better to think of staff governors as conduits of information between staff members and the governing body.

If a governor does want to find out more about your work in the school don't view the visit as an 'inspection'. He/she will simply be exploring the work of the school in action and will almost certainly be impressed with what goes on. Aim to include any visiting governors as much as possible and feel free to discuss the nitty-gritty of what you do.

You can find out more about the role of governing bodies here: www.governornet.co.uk.

Should TAs be invited to school functions?

Absolutely! Although you may not be employed full time, or be on the premises as much as other members of the school's community, you are as important as any other employee when it comes to such matters! It's really vital for schools to include TAs in such events and celebrations and many TAs find that the more they involve themselves in this side of school life, the more fulfilment they get out of the job. After all, this is a great way of finding out more about the people you work with and seeing them in contexts beyond the classroom. This all helps to develop working relationships and that has to be a positive thing.

Is it appropriate to socialise with teachers outside school?

Yes, absolutely! Many schools have teachers and TAs who socialise together and this can be great for team building. Don't ever feel obliged to socialise with work colleagues but if you do decide to you will almost certainly reap the benefits.

How can teachers and TAs best review their classroom relationship?

Regularly is the answer to that! The more often you do this the easier it will be to make the subtle alterations in your classroom practice that may be needed. TAs and teachers who achieve this effectively tend to review their progress through discussion, which enables both to focus on what they consider to be positive and what they consider might need further development.

Ultimately, you would want be aiming at identifying what you do well together and what might need further improvement. The 'two stars and a wish' approach works with adults too!

The teacher I work with has introduced 'report sheets' for me to complete at the end of each day. It's very time-consuming. Are they really such a good idea?

Report sheets can be a great way of keeping a written record of work achieved with a particular pupil, for example. This could come in very useful for inspection or internal appraisals of your work. The act of writing these notes down can also mean that you retain more information about a child and find it easier to pick up where you left off next time you see them.

If you are finding that they are taking too long to complete, talk about how the sheets might be streamlined before thinking about discussing abandoning the idea altogether. It's worth making them work if at all possible.

When I'm working with children with SEN should I be meeting with the school's SENCO on a regular basis too?

Ideally, yes, but this may not be formally organised. The chances are it will be a matter of having a quick chat when the need arises unless you decide between you that you need to be meeting to discuss work and perhaps plan and prepare classroom materials for a particular child. All of this depends on the working relationship you have with the teacher and the SENCO. There is no doubt that regular meetings with the SENCO will be incredibly helpful so if you feel that you would benefit from this, do ask the teacher and SENCO if something can be arranged on a regular basis.

I am bilingual and frequently find myself being called on to translate teaching materials and communications with parents. Is this reasonable?

If you feel as though you are being deployed in a way which differs from your job description, it would definitely be worth having a discussion with the headteacher. It could be that no one in the school realises how you feel about your skills being used in this way and it may be possible to negotiate additional pay or a revised job description.

It's very positive for schools to use the skills they have at their disposal, but it is important that you don't end up feeling 'put upon'. A quick discussion with the head will usually clear up such a matter.

CHAPTER 9

Career development

Your talent determines what you can do. Your motivation determines how much you are willing to do. Your attitude determines how well you do it.

(Lou Holtz)

Introduction

Even if you simply want to stand still in your career, you have to develop! There is no such thing as treading water. Keeping your job ticking over so that you are as effective as you can be as a TA requires your commitment to noticing what's new out there and what could usefully inform your work in the classroom. Think of the bees . . . when a new source of pollen is found, most of the bees in a hive fly to it while, say, 20 per cent of the bees check out where even newer sources of pollen can be found. And that should be your attitude to your job: 80 per cent of your focus could be on doing what gets results in the classroom, while 20 per cent could be focusing on development and expansion.

Career development is not necessarily about taking courses and striving for new positions of greater responsibility, although it can be. Professional development can be as simple as learning to be a reflective practitioner in the classroom. Being open to recognising that it's not just the pupils who learn in a classroom, TAs and teachers do too, can be a huge step towards ensuring that professional learning is a way of life for you at school.

FAQs in this chapter cover:

- Making progress as a TA
- Gaining qualifications
- Studying to progress
- Appraisal as a TA
- Continuing professional development
- Carrying out research projects
- Doing a skills audit
- Higher level teaching assistants:

    - Background to the role
    - Training
    - Steps to becoming an HLTA
    - Funding
    - Professional standards for HLTAs
    - Assessment for HLTA status
    - HLTAs in schools
    - Pay and as HLTA
    - HLTA roles
    - HLTA status as a stepping stone to QTS
    - QTS as an HLTA

- Professional development portfolios

I don't particularly want to be a 'career TA'. I just enjoy my job and I'm happy doing what I'm doing right now. Do I have to 'make progress'?

If you work with commitment you will 'make progress' whether you like it or not! Just by gaining work experience on the job you will develop professionally and progress. That said, there is absolutely nothing wrong with wanting to consolidate what you do in the classroom. There are no unwritten rules suggesting that all TAs must strive to be 'career TAs' so if your goal is to learn the craft and perform that role to the best of your ability that is perfectly acceptable.

As long as you are open to new learning as it arises and when necessary, you will be fine. Become closed to development opportunities, however, and you risk becoming stale and your effectiveness in the classroom will undoubtedly suffer. You will be a stronger professional if you are aware of all the development opportunities that arise during the course of your work in the classroom.

I've been doing my job as a TA for a year now so is it necessary for me to do any qualifications? Surely my experience on the job is enough?

You're right, your experience on the job is adequate now that you are already in employment. But if you want to change jobs or develop your role further in school, you may find that the process of studying for additional qualifications is very supportive of your goals.

Aim not to think of any qualifications that you may choose to study for as a chore. Invariably they will lead to renewed interest in your role in school and the chances are you'll develop contacts in other schools that could greatly support your work.

> If you are unsure as to whether further training and development would benefit you, talk to your class teacher and/or headteacher for advice. You may also want to make sure that this issue is included in any appraisals that you have at school.

Although I am a TA already, I would like to do something to gain formal qualifications to stand me in good stead to progress. What should my next step be?

It is great to think ahead about what you may want to do in the future and to plan your studies accordingly. There are several options open to you. Try these for starters:

- Speak to your headteacher about training and development opportunities in the local area, perhaps being run by the local authority, that you could participate in.
- Contact your local further education college to see if it is running any NVQs for TAs that you can study for.
- Consider becoming an HLTA (see page 133).
- Contact Learndirect (www.learndirect.co.uk) for information on suitable courses and learning for your skills and experience.
- You may want to think about becoming a specialist in a particular learning difficulty or special educational need. Your headteacher will be able to discuss this possibility with you in more depth.

There are growing numbers of fully interactive online courses for TAs to complete. The Learndirect website has more information on this, as do sites such as that offered by Optimus Professional Learning, which carries courses for TAs on developing skills. Visit www.learndirect.co.uk and www.optimusprolearning.com for more details.

Will I be appraised as a TA?

Yes, you should be. You are entitled to development in your job and in order to assess your development needs your line manager and/or headteacher will want to review your progress and performance on a regular basis.

The generally held belief is that the skills of an effective TA can be taught, so while all TAs will perform their roles differently, the core skills involved are thought to be identifiable and teachable where necessary.

Any appraisal of your work should be done in the spirit of recognising your strengths and identifying your development needs. It is not solely about seeing what you need to do 'better'. A good appraisal is a dialogue between you and your appraiser. It is most certainly a two-way process and not simply a series of statements made about your work. Appraisals should be done on a regular basis (usually annually). It is likely that your job description will be used as one basis for your appraisal and it could be that this changes as a result of exploring the work you undertake in school as part of your appraisal.

Appraisals typically explore the work of a TA in terms of the support he/she provides for the pupils and for the teacher(s) he/she works with. They may also go into the support the TA provides for the curriculum being taught and for the school as a whole to the extent that this is detailed in the TA's job description. Any areas for development that are identified should relate directly to the work the TA is employed to do.

Part of any appraisal process that you go through should also include the opportunity to discuss your career aspirations and the current possibilities open to you. You should also discuss the progress you have made since the last appraisal and for this reason it is wise to keep track of any developments as they happen. You may want to use your professional development portfolio for this purpose. Finally, the date of the next appraisal should be set (or at least agreed in principle) and you should have the opportunity to see and approve any written record of the appraisal process you go through.

> You can find out more about how appraisals are undertaken in your school from your headteacher. If you have any concerns at all about this aspect of the job, don't hesitate to ask. Appraisal is not intended to be a tool of discipline. Rather, it is a method for finding out what you're doing well, and what aspects of the job might see you benefit from support.

Is CPD only about going on courses? If so, will I get the opportunity to go on some?

While you should get the opportunity to attend necessary courses to enhance your development as a TA, CPD is much more than this.

There are numerous sources of professional development in schools for TAs. For example:

- keeping a professional diary or journal
- observing colleagues, teachers and TAs alike
- carrying out research
- visiting other schools
- doing a self-appraisal
- having professional discussions with colleagues
- mentoring new staff
- devising additional resources
- sharing good practice
- reading about issues connected with your work
- evaluating your classroom practice
- becoming a school governor.

Being aware of all the many opportunities for development that exist throughout the course of the usual school day means that you are more likely to take those opportunities and fully incorporate professional learning into each and every day.

Your headteacher will be able to talk to you about your entitlement to CPD and training. If you have identified a particular course that you feel would be helpful for you improving your classroom work, it is perfectly acceptable to talk to the head or the person with responsibilities for staff professional development about the possibility of you attending.

I would like to carry out a small research project in my school but I'm not entirely sure how to go about it. What should I do?

It can be incredibly useful for TAs to undertake research projects in schools, either as teams or as individuals. There are a number of steps that can be taken. These ideas should help:

- Establish a focus for your research and write down a statement of intent describing what it is that you intend to learn from the research.
- Talk to your headteacher and the teacher(s) you work with about your ideas.
- Make a list of all the possible sources of help that are available to you (again, discussing this with the head is bound to be fruitful).
- Plan carefully and precisely how you will be carrying out the research, including making a list of all the resources (don't forget time as a resource!) that you will require.
- When you are carrying out the research make sure that you monitor your progress closely. In particular you need to aim to identify unintended or unexpected outcomes.
- Take time to reflect on the evidence that you have gained. What have you learned? How reliable is the evidence you have gathered? What impact has it had?
- Put the research in context and consider what it might lead to in the future.
- Identify any changes that need to take place in response to your research.

I would like to think about the training needs that I might have but I'm not sure how to go about structuring this. Where should I start?

Doing a skills audit is always a good idea when you are thinking about CPD. You may like to consider your skills in relation to the following areas of your work:

- numeracy
- literacy
- SEN
- behaviour management
- ICT skills
- study skills
- thinking skills

- specific curriculum subject areas
- working with teachers
- working with parents
- working with pupils.

These kinds of skills audits can either be for your eyes only or, perhaps more usefully, they can be used as a basis for discussion with the teacher(s) you work with or the headteacher. Showing that you are open to looking at your own skills openly and frankly, and that you do this proactively, will always go down well and may lead to additional support or training where necessary.

I've heard about HLTAs. Can anyone become one?

If you are working in England and your headteacher (or line manager) considers you to be suitable to become an HLTA, you can apply to your local authority with your headteacher's approval for a place on the programme.

How long do I need to have been a TA before I train to be an HLTA?

This depends entirely on your individual levels of motivation, competence, background and so on. That said, it is rare for TAs to move on to HLTA status within the first two years of work. HLTAs typically have had at least two years of classroom experience before taking that development step. But it is important to remember that there is no hard and fast rule about this. If you can meet all the standards for HLTAs (see page 162), then go for it. If you have no experience at all, it would be rare for you to be able to hit every HLTA standard consistently earlier than two years of experience.

What is the background to HLTA status?

The national agreement on raising standards and tackling workload, which was signed by the government, employers and some unions on

15 January 2003, introduced the idea that in order to tackle un-
acceptable workload levels managed by teachers, there would need
to be significant changes to their conditions of service. The agreement
also acknowledged the major role played by school support staff and
led to the creation of HLTA status among other new roles in schools
for those who support the work of teachers. The main contractual
changes brought in as a result of the agreement were organised
into three phases from September 2003 to September 2005.

As well as the development of HLTA status, the agreement recognised that there are occasions when teachers are not the most appropriate member of staff to undertake certain tasks. This led to the
creation and implementation of other support roles including cover
supervisors, pastoral managers and invigilation staff.

> There is more information on the national agreement on raising stan-
> dards and tackling workload on the TDA website: www.tda.gov.uk.

What are the main steps to becoming an HLTA?

Once you have decided to pursue becoming an HLTA, the TDA says
there are four steps to take:

- applying for funding
- training
- preparation for assessment
- assessment.

> You can find out all about these steps from the TDA website:
> www.tda.gov.uk.

Is there any funding available to help me to become an HLTA?

Yes there is funding available from local authorities (in the form of supply cover costs, travel and subsistence costs, childcare costs, etc.), but not all TAs will be eligible. If you are one who is not eligible, you will need to get funding from your school (some schools offer funding from their training budgets) or self-fund.

How do I go about applying for funding to become an HLTA?

First of all, you need to be employed in a school already as a TA and you need to have the backing of your headteacher or line manager. In other words, they need to agree that you are a suitable candidate to go for HLTA status.

The TDA allocates funding to local authorities for the HLTA programme. If you want to go for funding you would need to contact your local authority for details of their application process. These will be different in each area.

> The contact details for local authorities can be found in your Yellow Pages or on the TDA website: www.tda.gov.uk.

How do I know if it is worth me applying to become an HLTA?

A good way of assessing this is to take a look through the HLTA standards to see if you have the potential to meet them (see Appendix 1). These standards are what all candidates must have achieved by the end of their training. You will also need to ensure that you can provide evidence that you have literacy and numeracy qualifications to Level 2 of the National Qualifications Framework (for example, GCSE grades A*–C) in order to reach the stage where you are ready to prepare for assessment. You may also like to discuss this with the teacher(s) you work with and your headteacher. Their opinions will be valuable in these early stages and you need the backing of your headteacher and line manager when you apply to your local authority for funding.

For further information on the National Qualifications Framework, which is a framework of qualifications organised into eight levels to make it easier to see the level at which they should be recognised, take a look at the QCA website: www.qca.org.uk.

If you need further information about your qualifications or you want to find out about adult literacy and numeracy classes in your area (often these come under the heading 'Skills for Life') give Learndirect a call on 0800 100 900.

What do the professional standards for HLTA status cover?

There are 31 standards for HLTA status and they are organised under the following headings:

1   Professional values and practice.
2   Knowledge and understanding.
3   Teaching and learning activities.

See Appendix I for the standards for HLTA status in full.

I have already gained relevant NVQs for my job. Does that mean I'd be able to become an HLTA?

Yes, in theory it does, although you would still need to be assessed formally against the national standards for HLTAs. It is these standards that all potential HLTAs must meet by the time they reach the end of their training. The transition from TA to HLTA is not a foregone conclusion, although there's no reason why, with the right support and training, the standards can't be within reach.

Is the training the same for all of those going for HLTA status?

No it isn't. Your local authority will assess what training you need to move on to HLTA status in discussion with your school. Any training you are deemed to need will be specific to your circumstances and won't necessarily be the same as others going for HLTA status.

Will I have to go back to college to train to become an HLTA?

Not necessarily. Once your needs have been assessed you may be given activities to develop your skills within your school or it could be that your local authority provides training suitable for you to attend. Another possibility is that independent training providers offer what you need to bring your skills up to scratch for assessment against the standards for HLTA status.

> For details of local training opportunities contact your local authority or regional provider of assessment (RPA).

If I decided to go for HLTA status how would I prepare for assessment?

The TDA states that during the process of preparing for assessment you would receive up to three days of guidance and briefing so that you are completely certain how to go about succeeding in the assessment tasks. It recommends that your preparation for assessment should involve

- making sure that you understand the professional standards and how they relate to your work in school
- preparing for the four assessment tasks, which are used to record your achievement against the standards
- receiving formative feedback (feedback that is designed to improve your performance) on the assessment tasks
- preparing for the visit to your school by an assessor.

The TDA has additional information about preparation for assessment for HLTA status and in particular recommends downloading the *Assessment Forms for Candidates – F1–F9*, which can be found on the TDA website (look for the pages for support staff in the main menu): www.tda.gov.uk. It is important to do this as it helps you to determine where you are in the process.

When I am assessed for HLTA status, what will happen?

When you are assessed, an assessor will visit your school for half a day to go through your evidence that you meet the standards for HLTA status. During this visit you will have the opportunity to talk about the evidence you have used and the activities that support it. You'll be able to show any written evidence to back you up as well as having what you present to the assessor verified by your head-teacher and the class teacher(s) you work with. Once the visit from the assessor is over, he/she will have to make a decision on whether you should be deemed to have met the standards for HLTA status. The RPA will then let you know what the outcome is within eight weeks of the assessor's visit to your school.

> The TDA recommends that you read its *Handbook for candidates*, which can be downloaded from its website (go to the resources section): www.tda.gov.uk.

I'm nervous about the thought of assessment and can't imagine going through it. Is it really something to be nervous about?

No! It's an inevitable part of any developmental process and is important as a means of checking the level at which you're working. While it's natural to be nervous about this kind of assessment, especially if you're attached to a particular outcome, the more you can take it in your stride the easier the whole thing will be. You won't be going for assessment until you are ready and there is a very good chance of getting through, so take comfort from that. Very few people fail too!

> If nerves really are getting the better of you take some time to remember that you are perfectly capable of meeting the standards for HLTA status otherwise your headteacher would not have recommended you. Don't let a lack of confidence stand in the way of making progress. Talk to your class teacher or headteacher about your concerns sooner rather than later, listen to their advice and trust in your abilities.

If I go through the HLTA training and successfully meet all the standards in the assessment, will I actually be teaching in the classroom?

That depends entirely on how your headteacher wants to deploy you in his/her school. He/she will need to consider the school's needs and discuss these with other school staff as well as with you before drawing up a job description for you to work from.

The TDA says that the HLTA's role is to 'advance pupil learning in a range of classroom settings'. This means that you may be working with individuals, groups or whole classes depending on current need. If you have the right 'skills, expertise and experience' you may well be taking whole classes for *some* teaching and learning activities.

However, it is important to keep in mind that HLTAs are assistants working at a more independent level than other TAs who have not been through the assessment for HLTA status. It is not the role of HLTAs to replace teachers in classrooms. It is their role to assist teachers at a high level. You may be doing some work with whole classes but not all your work as an HLTA should be like this. Every class must still have a class teacher who is ultimately responsible for learning outcomes. This is an important point.

By way of an example of how HLTAs are already working, a document released by the Workforce Monitoring Group in June 2006 (Note 17, downloadable from the TDA website: www.tda.gov.uk) on the effective deployment of HLTAs in schools listed the following ideas:

- Working as organisers of a transition programme for pupils from pre-school to school, infant to junior or primary to secondary school.
- Devising learning plans for children with special educational needs to enable teaching colleagues to deliver more effective teaching, e.g. devising plans with a kinaesthetic approach.
- Working with pupils from different ethnic backgrounds and helping with the inclusion of children from very diverse backgrounds, thus creating positive relationships between home and school.
- Being responsible for ICT management; in collaboration with teachers, teaching whole classes on ICT and assessing pupils; giving information and advice on new ICT products; giving tailored ICT support for pupils with SEN.
- Developing a peer mediation system to tackle and resolve conflicts between pupils, and training pupil mediators.
- Putting together study guides on English novels for less able students in collaboration with teachers.
- Supporting pupils during the award scheme development and accreditation network scheme, which offers key vocational skills to those doing only core GCSE subjects by producing worksheets and giving general support.

- Acting as specialists in counselling and managing EBD [emotional and behavioural difficulties], provide team-teach training for colleagues working in pupil support centres.

But remember, it is up to your headteacher, the class teacher(s) you are working with and you to decide how best you should be deployed in your school. The above are just examples.

The resources for HLTAs and those thinking about training to become an HLTA are incredibly useful. You can find these here: www.tda.gov.uk/support/hlta/resourcebank.aspx.

How are HLTAs received in schools?

Evidence suggests that HLTAs are received really well in schools. Those that have them want more and more of them because they realise what a tremendous asset they are to the work of the school community. They operate at a higher level regarding pedagogy and subject knowledge and so on, and so they become highly valued members of teams. HLTAs generally work in ways in which TAs would not typically work. There are additional factors in terms of what they do during their working days and which teachers are getting to value immensely. For example, one HLTA in a primary school was given responsibility for religious education across the whole school. While she did not work autonomously, she used her knowledge of religious studies to help teachers to plan lessons and she delivered key points of learning herself. She worked with teachers in true partnership, as a team. The teachers, pupils and parents were very appreciative of what she did and the ways in which her expert skills and knowledge were utilised in the school. Having HLTA status really helped to facilitate that. There are many anecdotes like this all over the country describing how the approximately 13,000 (as of August 2006) HLTAs have crafted a role in schools using their expertise.

Will I be paid more as an HLTA?

It is impossible to give a categorical answer on this but the national agreement from which HLTA status emerged does recognise that support staff should be remunerated to reflect their level of training, skills and responsibilities. However, it is up to your school's governing body, in discussion with your headteacher, to determine what your rate of pay should be. The TDA has no remit or powers in respect of pay for HLTAs. It can advise and support where possible but it can't force schools to pay more for its HLTAs.

If you are unsure about the effect that having HLTA status will have on your pay, talk to your headteacher. If you would like advice from outside your school, you may want to contact your union.

If I gain HLTA status will I definitely be deployed in HLTA roles?

There is guidance to schools published by the union UNISON that states that those with HLTA status should be deployed in HLTA roles, but schools are still free to deploy support staff in the best way they see fit for their needs (within reason). This means that because of the variables involved, headteachers should be discussing with any TAs who gain HLTA status precisely what their new role in school will be, along with any implications for their timetable and job description. All of this should be agreed between the head and the HLTA.

Gaining HLTA status does not mean that you will be guaranteed a job as an HLTA. But you should not be expected to work at the higher level of an HLTA without being properly rewarded.

If you have any doubts or concerns about the way in which you are deployed as an HLTA in your school, talk to your union for clarification and advice.

Once I have become an HLTA what can I do next? Can I automatically become a qualified teacher?

No, not necessarily, although having HLTA status is likely to stand you in good stead for progressing on to QTS. If you want to become a fully qualified teacher you will need to apply for initial teacher training. There are several routes into teaching including school-based graduate and registered teacher programmes. These allow trainees to learn on the job and be paid as unqualified teachers at the same time. You may also want to consider the more traditional undergraduate and postgraduate courses.

There does seem to be a very natural progression from HLTA status to QTS. Approximately 25 per cent of HLTAs are, at the time of writing, either actively involved in training or say they will become involved in training for QTS. HLTA status is seen increasingly as a stepping stone from assisting in the classroom to operating as a fully qualified teacher. Without that stepping stone, the leap from TA to teacher may seem too great for some. As most TAs will know, teachers who have experience of assisting in the classroom often make the best use of their TAs!

If you do decide to take this route, there are no limits to what you could achieve in the profession. There are headteachers working in schools today who started their careers as TAs.

Everything you need to know about training to be a teacher can be found on the TDA website: www.tda.gov.uk. You may also like to read about being an NQT in *The Newly Qualified Teacher's Handbook* (Routledge, 2002) and *FAQs for NQTs* (Routledge, 2006).

I am a qualified teacher and have not been able to secure permanent employment as a teacher so I am thinking about becoming an HLTA so that I am still gaining classroom experience. As I already have QTS am I automatically an HLTA?

No. You would still have to go through the same assessment process as others seeking HLTA status. As you already have QTS you would almost certainly find this process relatively easy as you would be used to operating at or above this level in the classroom anyway. The standards for HLTA status are very closely aligned to the standards for QTS so there is a strong cross-referencing between the two. If you have QTS you would almost certainly be able to prove that you have the skills to become an HLTA, but you would need to go through the assessment process.

I've heard some of the teachers talk about their professional development portfolios but should I have one of those too? Is it necessary for TAs to have them?

There is no reason why TAs shouldn't have a professional development portfolio. Think of it as a working CV that carries examples of your practice in the classroom and concrete evidence of the way in which you support children's learning.

If you are starting to create a professional development portfolio, aim to contain it in a folder no bigger than A3 (A4 will be fine if you are not including larger items) and think about how you want to label the items you include. The best portfolios have a lot of attention to this kind of detail. Consider including these items (remember, there are no set rules on this, so just use this list as guidance):

- examples of any planning you have done for a child or children (you can still include examples of any co-planning you have done with the class teacher)

- examples of any lessons or parts of lessons that you have delivered
- photographs of children's work that was completed under your guidance
- something that shows that you are aware of current priorities in education (for example, some support materials you may have developed for literacy and numeracy work)
- examples of cross-curricular work with pupils, perhaps in ICT
- a record of your skills and attributes
- a record of your professional learning to date including a focus on areas of your work for future development
- a brief statement that outlines your personal philosophy of working as a TA – what is the mission statement that you work by? (Not the school's, but your own – something that stands you apart from other TAs.) You may want to draw on the National Standards to help you to write this.

You may want to create a pool of items that you can use to fill your portfolio in the event of going for a job interview. While it is still pretty rare to be asked for a professional development portfolio as a TA, there is no harm in being ahead of the crowd!

Above all else, a professional development portfolio can greatly enhance your self-esteem as a classroom professional as well as making applying for jobs in different schools easier. They are an excellent way of displaying your skills and experiences tangibly and visibly, and show your commitment to adopting a professional attitude to your work.

CHAPTER 10

Hot education topics

> Every job is a self-portrait of the person who does it. Autograph your work with excellence.
>
> (Unknown)

Introduction

As a TA you will be, or already are, part of a dynamic profession that must respond to a full range of external pressures, from parents' expectations to new initiatives from the government, from inspection to raising standards. Unless you are hooked to rolling news channels, or glued to the DfES website, you're unlikely to be bang up to date with what's going on all the time, but that needn't be a problem. There are plenty of ways of staying in touch with the wider picture in education without becoming a slave to your job!

This chapter explores some of the more dominant issues facing education in general and TAs in schools right now.

FAQs in this chapter cover:

- Ofsted inspection
- Reasons for inspection
- Features of inspection
- Inspection as a TA
- Supporting teachers through inspection
- Remaining calm through inspections

- Keeping up to date with education developments
- The national strategies for literacy and numeracy
- Inclusion
- *Every Child Matters*
- Extended schools
- Workforce remodelling
- Brain Gym ®
- Emotional literacy
- Creativity in the classroom
- Personalised learning
- National awards for TAs

What is inspection?

Inspection is the method by which the government gathers evidence on the quality of public services that are provided. School inspection provides such evidence and informs the approaches to caring for and supporting children that are adopted. It also provides information on the types of educational provision that are most effective.

Why are schools inspected?

Ofsted states in its literature: 'Inspection provides an independent, external evaluation of the effectiveness of a school in promoting the standards, personal development and well-being of its learners, the quality of its provision and how well it is led and managed.' It is part of the accountability process. Providing education costs the nation an immense amount of money and inspection is one way of finding out whether that money is being well spent. It is also a way of helping schools to improve the quality of the education they offer and of helping them to continue to raise standards. If one thing is certain in education, whoever is in power, it is that standards achieved must never be allowed to drift. The drive is constantly onwards and upwards. There are many positive aspects of inspection, not least the fact that schools can say to pupils and parents, look, this is what we do and this is what those outside our community think of what we are doing. It also enables government ministers to gather information on what's happening to the quality of education in schools and to make and change laws and guidance accordingly.

What are the main features of inspection?

From a TA's perspective, the features of inspection that you should be aware of include the following:

- There is a strong focus on pupil well-being during inspection in respect to the *Every Child Matters* agenda (see page 154). It is worth keeping this in mind given that the role of TA is often inextricably linked with the well-being of the children you work with.
- The notice that schools receive of an impending inspection is very short now. Typically schools are notified during the week before inspection starts.
- Inspectors are in school usually for no more than two days.
- Individual subjects are not inspected.
- Inspectors will respond to what they find in and on the school (for example, on examining the school's self-evaluation). This means that they are likely to be flexible in their approach to the inspection.
- Judgements made on standards and pupil progress will be based on performance data.
- The quality of teaching is judged through a range of factors, not just lesson observations.
- Inspections are designed to impact a school's improvement.
- The size of the inspection team and the time they spend in school depends on the size of the school and the extent of the services it provides.
- It is likely that not all teachers will be observed.
- Inspectors may attach to year groups in order to experience registration, for example, or circle time.

- The time that inspectors spend in school will be used to gather evidence. They do this by observing lessons, talking to staff (all kinds, possibly including TAs) and learners, exploring processes such as performance management in the school, analysing samples of work, sitting in on meetings, and analysing pupils' records (for example, those with SEN).
- Inspections are intended to be 'tightly focused and efficient' (Ofsted).
- Inspectors do not need to witness full lessons, although they may decide to do so.
- Inspectors will generally spend half an hour in each lesson they visit (although, sometimes more, sometimes less!).
- Inspectors will talk to pupils during the inspection.
- The five outcomes of *Every Child Matters* will receive particular focus in inspections (see page 154).
- Inspectors may focus on case studies of vulnerable children (either those who are looked after by the local authority or those with learning difficulties and disabilities). If you work with one of these as a TA you may be called on to talk to inspectors.
- Inspectors will be exploring evidence of pupils' personal development and well-being as well as achievement and attainment.
- As well as looking at curriculum delivery and enrichment, inspectors will be looking at how well learners are cared for, guided and supported.

> You can find out all you need to know about inspections and their possible outcomes from the Ofsted website: www.ofsted.gov.uk. You can also contact the enquiry line on: 08456 404045.

If Ofsted comes to my school will I be inspected as a TA?

No, not as such. The best way to think about inspection as a TA is that you are part of a whole school community that is being inspected.

You can find out all you need to know about inspection as a TA from the Ofsted website: www.ofsted.gov.uk.

How can I support the teacher I work with through an inspection?

Inspection is not about endless preparation and paperwork. It is about showing inspectors the actual work of a school, as it happens day after day, term after term. It isn't about putting on a show, but it is about showing what you do and making explicit what is implicit in the functions of the school community. With this in mind, the best way you can support a teacher through inspection is to do what you usually do!

That said, there may be key aspects of planning and preparation that the teacher may require additional assistance with, not to mention general preparation of the teaching space. Although inspectors don't want to see anything special being laid on, it is only natural for a teacher to want to show inspectors the best of what happens in their classroom. In addition, you may need to be a little more flexible during the inspection period in case there are any last-minute needs. That's all a teacher would ask of their TA at such a time and any such flexibility is likely to be warmly appreciated.

If it is likely that Ofsted will be paying a visit to your school in the foreseeable future, it would be worth taking the time to discuss with the teacher(s) you work with exactly how you can best support them at this time. It is far better to have talked this through in advance than waiting until the school is notified before even thinking about how you might best work together to give inspectors the best impression of what you do.

How can I remain as calm as possible through an inspection?

There really is no need at all to let the prospect of an inspection stress you in any way. They are a fact of school life, we all know that they will take place even if we now get very little notice of when, and schools that are functioning well and effectively will have their efforts recognised and those that could do with some development guidance are likely to receive it. The reality of inspection is that there is very little to get concerned about, especially from the perspective of a TA. They are not inherently stressful events!

The best thing you can do is to read up about inspection so that you know exactly what the process is that the school will go through. Knowledge is power in this situation as fear of the unknown can lead to unnecessary stress. Second, talk to the teacher(s) you work with so that you are fully aware of the expectations of you once the inspectors arrive. Finally, treat the inspection like any other working day; there is no need for anything else.

How can I best keep up to date with what's going on in the world of education given that I don't have much spare time?

It's difficult when you are working part time or when your life is busy and full to keep track of exactly what is going on in the world of education and everything that might have an impact on your work in schools. Fortunately this needn't be a problem. These ideas for keeping up to date may help:

- Your school first and foremost should inform you of any significant changes and developments in education that you should know about.
- The BBC website has an extensive education news area that carries the very latest stories and information about the profession: www.bbc.co.uk.

- The DfES website naturally carries all the latest government news for education. You can find it here: www.dfes.gov.uk.
- TeacherNet is the government's website for teachers and other school staff. It carries a huge amount of news, resources and articles among other things, which you can find here: www.teachernet.gov.uk.
- Teachers' TV is a television channel for teachers and other school staff. The website is worth browsing, even if you don't get a chance to watch the channel: www.teachers.tv.
- There are some local and national publications (both in paper form and online) for TAs. Some of these are produced by local authorities or higher education institutions and some are priced publications such as the magazine *Learning Support*. Take a look at www.learningsupport.co.uk for further information.
- Many of the national newspapers carry education news stories and some, for example, the *Independent*, the *Guardian* and *The Times*, have education supplements which may be of interest.
- Your school may subscribe to professional journals for staff members. These would normally be found in staffrooms. Look out too for any TA-specific literature prepared by your union. Again, this would often be placed in staffrooms if not sent directly to your home.

Don't get hung up on trying to keep as up to date as possible. Yes, it is important to be clued up to an extent, but your school should ensure that you don't operate in a vacuum and should let you know all the crucial information you need to know.

I have heard about the national strategies for numeracy and literacy. What exactly are they and how can I find out more about them?

These national strategies for literacy and numeracy set out teaching objectives from reception to Year 6 to help enable pupils to become fully numerate and literate. Your school will be able to offer further information on the way in which these strategies are implemented and your role as a TA in supporting them.

> These national strategies have now been taken under the wing of the Primary National Strategy. This is all about raising standards right across the whole curriculum. You can find out more about the Primary National Strategy from the Standards website: www.standards.dfes.gov.uk.

What is inclusion?

Inclusion refers to the entitlement that all children, including those from overseas and those with diverse learning needs, have to a broad and balanced curriculum. In reality, this means that mainstream schools typically accept a full range of pupils, some of whom may have specific learning or physical needs. Inclusion is not specific to particular subjects. It operates right across the curriculum.

> You can find out more about inclusion from the QCA and Standards websites: www.qca.org.uk and www.standards.dfes.gov.uk.

Am I likely to work with gifted and talented young people?

Some schools like to adopt the idea that *all* children are gifted and talented so if you work in such a school, yes you will! More typically, though, schools identify pupils who may be deemed 'gifted and talented learners' and may well decide to deploy TAs to help these young people to develop their skills further.

> Find out more about your school's approach to gifted and talented learners by speaking to the teacher(s) you work with and the head-teacher. The school should have a policy on how best to support these learners.

I understand that there is an **Every Child Matters** agenda. What is this?

Every Child Matters: Change for Children is described as 'a new approach to the wellbeing of children and young people from birth to age 19'. The government's aim is that each child will have the support they need to achieve the five outcomes listed below. TAs and other support staff are considered to be vital in carrying forward the intended outcomes of the *Every Child Matters* agenda.

Every Child Matters also features in Ofsted inspections, when inspectors will be looking for evidence that schools are helping pupils to achieve the five outcomes with which *Every Child Matters* is concerned. The following has been taken from the Ofsted document, *Conducting the Inspection: Guidance for Inspectors of Schools* (2005). The five outcomes are:

- Be healthy: for example helping learners to adopt healthy lifestyles, build their self-esteem, eat and drink well and lead active lives
- Stay safe: for example keeping learners safe from bullying, harassment and other dangers
- Enjoy and achieve: for example enabling learners to make good progress in their work and personal development and to enjoy their education

- Make a positive contribution: for example ensuring that learners understand their rights and responsibilities, are listened to, and participate in the life of the community
- Achieve economic wellbeing: for example helping pupils to gain the skills and knowledge needed for future employment.

Looking at this list it is easy to see that TAs can have an incredibly powerful impact on each one of those outcomes, and could usefully keep them in mind throughout all of their work in schools.

> You can find out more about *Every Child Matters* here: www. everychildmatters.gov.uk.

What are extended schools?

Extended schools are schools that provide 'a range of services and activities often beyond the school day to help meet the needs of its pupils, their families and the wider community' (DfES press release). They are thought to be a key way of delivering the *Every Child Matters* agenda and extended services provided typically include:

- childcare 8 a.m.–6 p.m. all year round
- parenting and family support
- study support, sport and music clubs
- community use of facilities such as ICT.

In the primary sector the notion of the extended school means:

- a range of study support activities: sports, arts, music, home-work, clubs, etc.
- parenting support opportunities, including family learning
- swift and easy referral from every school to a range of support services for children

- childcare available at least 8 a.m.–6 p.m. term time and during school holidays.

In the secondary phase, extended school means:

- study support activities: arts, music, opportunities to complete homework or coursework
- parenting support opportunities, including family learning
- swift and easy referral from every school to a range of specialised pupil support services
- scope for multi-agency teams on site
- opening up ICT, sports and arts facilities for use by the wider community.

It is thought that these services will improve pupil attendance, self-confidence and motivation and have a positive impact on achievement. Teachers too should be better enabled to focus on teaching and learning, and the services offered to children and their families should be enhanced.

> You can find out more about extended schools from TeacherNet: www.teachernet.gov.uk and from the schools remodelling website (part of the TDA website): www.remodelling.org.

What is workforce remodelling all about?

Workforce remodelling is all about how schools can introduce new ways of working as communities in order to bring benefits to pupils and the whole school team. It is a process of change 'which enables schools and other organisations to develop effective and long-term change programmes that meet their own specific circumstances' (www.tda.gov.uk).

In addition to managing change, workforce remodelling is also about the National Workload Agreement (see page 8) and extended schools.

As well as having an impact on the *Every Child Matters* agenda, TAs are also thought to be crucial to ensuring the success of the workforce remodelling that is currently going on in schools. In addition, new career pathways and developments for TAs are bound to emerge and be underpinned by revised national professional standards and qualifications.

> You can find out all you need to know about school workforce remodelling from the remodelling website (part of the TDA website): www.remodelling.org.

What is Brain Gym®?

Brain Gym® is described as a movement-based educational programme. It seeks to bring together the brain, senses and body so that the person doing it is ready to learn as effectively as possible. It is sometimes known as educational kinesiology and is certainly gaining popularity in the UK. Particularly if you are working in a primary school you are almost certain to come across it. Brain Gym® is said to help children to improve their academic skills, memory and concentration, physical coordination and balance and self-development among other things.

It would be worth asking the teacher(s) you work with if the school has a policy on using this technique with children. There may be resources and ideas already in place that you can utilise.

> You can find out more about Brain Gym® in the UK from the following website: www.braingym.org.uk.

The teacher I am working with is very keen on emotional literacy in the classroom. What should I know about this?

Emotional literacy has been defined by Antidote (see below) as: 'The practice of interacting with others in ways that build understanding of our own and others' emotions, then using this understanding to inform our actions.'

Some schools have a whole school policy on emotional literacy while in other schools it is very much down to individual teachers to focus on emotional literacy in their classrooms. Either way, schools can be particularly effective in developing young people's emotional literacy through close attention to relationships between pupils, between teachers and other school staff (such as TAs) and pupils, and between the adults in a school community.

An emotionally literate school is not one in which cross words are never uttered, or emotions don't run high from time to time. Rather, it is one where the feelings of each member of the community are fully appreciated and taken into consideration as far as possible. When disagreements do take place, they are dealt with effectively and learned from for the future.

> You can find out much more about emotional literacy and what it means in schools from the Antidote website: www.antidote.org.uk. Antidote was set up, according to its website, by a diverse group who set to 'apply the latest understandings of human nature to the challenge of creating a healthier and more sustainably prosperous society'.

I keep hearing about creativity in the classroom but I'm not sure what it means in practice. Any ideas?

There is no doubt that creativity in the classroom continues to be a buzz issue and it seems to have become synonymous with encouraging excellence through a wide range of activities linked to curriculum areas. It is about teaching through, for example, alternative methodologies, drama techniques, artwork, music as well as the more traditional methods for imparting knowledge and skills. The key is to consider what might encourage risk-taking, innovation, imagination, invention, originality and so on.

The National Curriculum in Action website states that creativity in the classroom is important because it helps pupils to think creatively and independently and to become

- more interested in discovering things for themselves
- more open to new ideas
- keen to work with others to explore ideas
- willing to work beyond lesson time when pursuing an idea or vision.

Creativity is thought to improve pupils' self-esteem as well as their levels of achievement and attainment. For this reason, a focus on creativity in the classroom is thought to be an incredibly enriching thing for teachers, support staff and their pupils.

What is personalised learning all about?

Personalised learning is part of a wider government strategy of personalisation across all of the public services. In short, as far as education is concerned, it's about helping children to reach their full potential within the learning context they find themselves in.

It is important to remember that personalised learning isn't individualised learning or one-to-one tuition, but it is about the way in which pupils learn as individuals who are part of a class. In short, personalised learning is learning that meets the needs of pupils.

> You can find out more about personalised learning either from the teacher(s) you work with or from the Standards website: www. standards.dfes.gov.uk.

I've heard that there are national awards for TAs. Is this true?

Yes there are National Awards for School Support Staff organised by UNISON in partnership with the GMB (a general union that anyone can join), the National Bursars Association and the National Governors Council. The awards given reflect the variety of work done by school support staff. Nominations are made each year ahead of the awards, which are given in eight categories:

- admin worker
- bursar
- catering worker
- premises worker
- pupil supervisor
- teaching assistant
- school cleaner
- technician.

There is also an award open to all types of TAs in the Teaching Awards. The specific criteria for that category are:

- demonstrates high aspirations for each pupil, a firm belief in pupils' abilities and a strong commitment to pupils' progress
- collaborates with teachers to establish clearly how they can each support individual pupils
- actively engages others in supporting pupils' learning and development, including parents, teachers and other professionals
- supports pupils in pursuit of clear goals even when the challenge is great or the outcome seems uncertain
- shows a continuing commitment to his or her own professional learning and personal development
- contributes to the whole staff team.

If nothing else, these criteria can be helpful in assessing your own performance at work. Could you tick all of those boxes?!

You can find out more about the nomination and award process for the National Awards for School Support Staff from the UNISON website: www.unison.org.uk. Information about the Teaching Awards can be found here: www.teachingawards.com.

The professional standards for HLTAs

The professional standards for HLTAs set out exactly what is expected of TAs who are working towards HLTA status.

The standards were developed by the TDA following a wide-ranging consultation with headteachers, teachers, professional bodies, unions, employers and support staff. There are 31 standards, grouped under three headings:

1   Professional values and practice.
2   Knowledge and understanding.
3   Teaching and learning activities

The standards, foreword and introduction have been reproduced here with the permission of the TDA and they can be found on the TDA website: www.tda.gov.uk/support/hlta/professstandards.aspx along with the document, *Guidance to the Standards*.

Foreword

Schools are changing. Headteachers and teachers know that the school workforce needs to be able to take its part in leading this change.

In January 2003, local employers, school workforce unions and the Department for Education and Skills (DfES) signed a national agreement that paved the way for radical reform of the school workforce to raise standards and tackle workload. This agreement included proposals to introduce the role of higher level teaching assistants (HLTA) who would bring a distinct contribution to the work of schools. Support for these proposals was very encouraging and the DfES and the Teacher Training Agency – now the Training and Development Agency for Schools (TDA) – published a set of national standards for higher level teaching assistants. This document sets out what is expected of those who are seeking to take on this additional responsibility. These standards help to ensure that all higher level teaching assistants have the necessary skills and expertise to make an active contribution to pupils' learning.

This is an exciting time to be working in schools: standards are rising; there are more teachers and support staff employed than ever before; teaching quality has never been better; there is greater community involvement; and time is being found for teachers to focus more closely on their professional role. We believe these standards reflect the high expectations the education sector has for all those who work in this role in schools, and that they will play their part in further embedding the role of the higher level teaching assistant in our schools.

Introduction

Support staff in schools make a strong contribution to pupils' learning and achievement. The national agreement between government, employers and school workforce unions has created the conditions in which teachers and support staff can work together even more effectively in professional teams. In this context, some support staff – HLTAs – are able to undertake a more extended role. The professional standards contained in this document set out the expectations of support staff who are identified as being able to work at this level.

Teachers' professional training, knowledge and experience prepare them to take overall responsibility for pupils' learning. However, they are not required to take sole responsibility for every aspect of each lesson that is taught. There are times when they will want to draw upon support from a wide range of other colleagues, including HLTAs.

The work of HLTAs complements that of teachers and the roles are not interchangeable. As more HLTAs have been trained and assessed as having met the standards, the range of support available to teachers and schools has been enhanced, allowing qualified teachers to make even more effective use of their time and their particular professional knowledge, skills and understanding.

HLTAs work in a range of different settings and with more autonomy than most other school support staff. Teachers and headteachers, working within the regulatory framework,[1] will be expected to make professional judgements about which teaching and learning activities HLTAs should undertake and what support and guidance they should have. These standards, and the associated training and assessment, are designed to provide assurance to teachers, employers and parents about the quality of contribution to pupils' learning that HLTAs can be expected to make.

The standards for HLTAs

These standards set out what an individual should know, understand and be able to do to be awarded HLTA status. They are organised in three inter-related sections:

Professional values and practice

These standards set out the attitudes and commitment to be expected from those trained as HLTAs.

Knowledge and understanding

These standards require HLTAs to demonstrate they have sufficient knowledge, expertise and awareness of the pupils' curriculum to work effectively with teachers as part of a professional team. They also require HLTAs to demonstrate that they know how to use their skills, expertise and experience to advance pupils' learning.

Teaching and learning activities

These standards require all HLTAs to demonstrate that they can work effectively with individual pupils, small groups and whole classes under the direction and supervision of a qualified teacher, and that they can contribute to a range of teaching and learning activities in the areas where they have expertise. They require all HLTAs to demonstrate skills in planning, monitoring, assessment and class management.

The standards apply to HLTAs working in all phases of education and in all areas of school life. They are designed to be applicable to the diversity of roles in which school support staff work to support pupils' learning. The standards complement those for qualified teacher status (QTS) enabling schools and candidates to see the relationship between the role of teachers and that of staff working at the higher level. HLTAs who wish to progress to QTS will have a clearer understanding of the additional knowledge and skills required.

Guidance to the standards

An accompanying booklet, *Guidance to the Standards*, helps to explain the knowledge and skills required by those seeking to demonstrate they have met the HLTA standards. It sets out the kind of evidence that would show that the standards have been met and the contexts in which this evidence is likely to be found. It also outlines the scope of each standard, and sets out the range of experiences, knowledge and activities that an individual may need to cover before being able to demonstrate that a standard has been met. Where relevant, the guidance indicates what falls outside the scope of a standard. The guidance is designed to help those who assess individuals against the standards, though it may be useful to headteachers and others with an interest in the work of HLTAs. The guidance aims to promote consistency of interpretation of the standards regardless of the context in which an HLTA works and is assessed.

Training for HLTAs

Support staff wishing to achieve HLTA status but who need to gain more knowledge, experience and skills relevant to, and related to, the standards should use the training opportunities available locally. This will be through their school, local authority (LA) or independent training providers. Candidates' prior achievements, experience of working in schools[2] and previous training could provide a firm foundation for their HLTA work. For support staff working in maintained schools, funding is available from the LA.

Regional providers of assessment (RPAs) or local authorities will be able to provide details of local provision. Contact details for the RPA in your region are available from www.tda.gov.uk/support/hlta/resourcebank

While the standards are generic across all key stages, training will provide opportunities for participants to build on and develop their prior specialist knowledge and experience, for example in individual subject areas, behaviour management, pastoral care, early years or special educational needs. Training will be tailored to meet the candidate's individual needs identified by a training needs analysis. All training will be related to one or more of the HLTA standards. Although training is likely to vary, all candidates will undergo the same HLTA preparation and assessment process. Assessment will require participants to apply their training to their own situation and will take place in the context of their specific specialist area.

The standards for HLTAs

1 Professional values and practice

Those meeting the higher level teaching assistant standards must demonstrate all of the following.

1.1

They have high expectations of all pupils; respect their social, cultural, linguistic, religious and ethnic backgrounds; and are committed to raising their educational achievement.

1.2

They build and maintain successful relationships with pupils, treat them consistently, with respect and consideration, and are concerned for their development as learners.

1.3

They demonstrate and promote the positive values, attitudes and behaviour they expect from the pupils with whom they work.

1.4

They work collaboratively with colleagues, and carry out their roles effectively, knowing when to seek help and advice.

1.5

They are able to liaise sensitively and effectively with parents and carers, recognising their roles in pupils' learning.

1.6

They are able to improve their own practice, including through observation, evaluation and discussion with colleagues.

2 Knowledge and understanding

Higher level teaching assistants (HLTAs) must demonstrate sufficient knowledge and understanding to be able to help the pupils they work with make progress with their learning. This knowledge and understanding will relate to a specialist area which could be subject-based or linked to a specific role (e.g. in support of an age phase or pupils with particular needs).

Those meeting the higher level teaching assistant standards must demonstrate all of the following.

2.1

They have sufficient understanding of their specialist area to support pupils' learning, and are able to acquire further knowledge to contribute effectively and with confidence to the classes in which they are involved.

2.2

They are familiar with the school curriculum, the age-related expectations of pupils, the main teaching methods and the testing/examination frameworks in the subjects and age ranges in which they are involved.

2.3

They understand the aims, content, teaching strategies and intended outcomes for the lessons in which they are involved, and understand the place of these in the related teaching programme.

2.4

They know how to use ICT to advance pupils' learning, and can use common ICT tools for their own and pupils' benefit.

2.5

They know the key factors that can affect the way pupils learn.

2.6

They have achieved a qualification in English/literacy and mathematics/numeracy, equivalent to at least level 2 of the National Qualifications Framework.

2.7

They are aware of the statutory frameworks relevant to their role.

2.8

They know the legal definition of Special Educational Needs (SEN), and are familiar with the guidance about meeting SEN given in the SEN Code of Practice.

2.9

They know a range of strategies to establish a purposeful learning environment and to promote good behaviour.

3 Teaching and learning activities

The following teaching and learning activities should take place under the direction and supervision of a qualified teacher in accordance with arrangements made by the headteacher of the school.

Those meeting the higher level teaching assistant standards must demonstrate all of the following.

3.1 Planning and expectations

3.1.1
They contribute effectively to teachers' planning and preparation of lessons.

3.1.2
Working within a framework set by the teacher, they plan their role in lessons including how they will provide feedback to pupils and colleagues on pupils' learning and behaviour.

3.1.3
They contribute effectively to the selection and preparation of teaching resources that meet the diversity of pupils' needs and interests.

3.1.4
They are able to contribute to the planning of opportunities for pupils to learn in out-of-school contexts, in accordance with school policies and procedures.

3.2 Monitoring and assessment

3.2.1
They are able to support teachers in evaluating pupils' progress through a range of assessment activities.

3.2.2
They monitor pupils' responses to learning tasks and modify their approach accordingly.

3.2.3
They monitor pupils' participation and progress, providing feedback to teachers, and giving constructive support to pupils as they learn.

3.2.4
They contribute to maintaining and analysing records of pupils' progress.

3.3 Teaching and learning activities

3.3.1
Using clearly structured teaching and learning activities, they interest and motivate pupils, and advance their learning.

3.3.2
They communicate effectively and sensitively with pupils to support their learning.

3.3.3
They promote and support the inclusion of all pupils in the learning activities in which they are involved.

3.3.4
They use behaviour management strategies, in line with the school's policy and procedures, which contribute to a purposeful learning environment.

3.3.5
They advance pupils' learning in a range of classroom settings, including working with individuals, small groups and whole classes where the assigned teacher is not present.

3.3.6
They are able, where relevant, to guide the work of other adults supporting teaching and learning in the classroom.

3.3.7
They recognise and respond effectively to equal opportunities issues as they arise, including by challenging stereotyped views, and by

challenging bullying or harassment, following relevant policies and procedures.

3.3.8
They organise and manage safely the learning activities, the physical teaching space and resources for which they are given responsibility.

Notes

1 For further details see the regulations and guidance under Section 133 of the Education Act 2002.
2 In this document, the term 'schools' includes mainstream schools, further education and sixth form colleges, early years settings, pupil referral units, and special schools where aspiring HLTAs can demonstrate that they meet the standards.

APPENDIX 2

Jargon buster

The jargon buster contains many of the acronyms commonly used in education, some of which are used in this book.

ACE	Advisory Centre for Education www.ace-ed.org.uk
ACE	Arts Council for England www.artscouncil.org.uk
ACPC	Area Child Protection Committee
ACW	Arts Council for Wales www.acw-ccc.org.uk
ADHD	attention deficit hyperactivity disorder
AEB	Associated Examining Board www.aeb.org.uk
AGCAS	Association of Graduate Careers Advisory Services www.agcas.org.uk/
AHRB	Arts and Humanities Research Board www.ahrb.ac.uk/
AHT	assistant headteachers
ALS	additional literacy support
AP	action plan
APL	accreditation of prior learning
APS	Alliance of Parents and Schools
AQA	Assessment and Qualifications Alliance www.aqa.org.uk
ASD	autistic spectrum disorder www.nas.org.uk
AST	advanced skills teacher www.standards.dfes.gov.uk/ast/
AT	attainment target
ATL	Association of Teachers and Lecturers www.askatl.org.uk

BEACO	behaviour and attendance coordinator (in secondary schools)
BECTA	British Educational Communication and Technology Agency www.becta.org.uk
BESTS	behaviour education support teams www.dfes.gov.uk/behaviourandattendance
BETT	British education and teaching technology www.becta.org.uk/
BIP	behaviour improvement programme
BSA	Basic Skills Agency www.basic-skills.co.uk
BSP	behaviour support plan
CAA	computer assisted assessment
CAL	computer assisted learning
CAMHS	Child and Adolescent Mental Health Services www.youngminds.org.uk/camhs/
CAT	cognitive ability test
CBEVE	Central Bureau for Educational Visits and Exchanges
CDC	Council for Disabled Children www.ncb.org.uk/cdc/
CEDC	Community Education Development Centre www.continyou.org.uk/
CEDP	Career Entry and Development Profile
CEG	careers education and guidance
CEO	chief education officer
CILT	Centre for Information on Language Teaching and Research www.cilt.org.uk/
CLPE	Centre for Language in Primary Education www.clpe.co.uk/
CPD	continuing professional development
CPI	child protection issue
CRAC	Careers Research and Advisory Centre www.crac.org.uk/
CRB	Criminal Records Bureau www.crb.gov.uk/
CRE	Commission for Racial Equality www.cre.gov.uk/
C School	county school
CTC	city technology college

D&T	design and technology
DENI	Department of Education for Northern Ireland www.deni.gov.uk/
DfES	Department for Education and Skills www.dfes.gov.uk/
DHT	deputy headteacher
DLO	desirable learning outcome
DPC	Data Protection Commission www.informationcommissioner.gov.uk/
DRC	Disability Rights Commission www.drc-gb.org/
EA	external assessor
EAL	English as an additional language
EAZ	education action zone
EBD	emotional and behavioural difficulties
EBP	education business partnership
EDP	education development plan
Edubase	database of educational establishments in England and Wales www.edubase.gov.uk/Index.aspx
EEC	early excellence centre www.literacytrust.org.uk/Database/earlyex.html
EFL	English as a foreign language
EFS	educational formula spending
EHWB	emotional health and well-being
EiC	Excellence in Cities www.standards.dfes.gov.uk/sie/eic/
ELC	eLearning Credit
ELG	early learning goal
ELWa	Education and Learning Wales www.elwa.org.uk/
EMA	education maintenance allowance
ERIC	everyone reading in class
ESL	English as a second language
ESO	education supervision order
ESOL	English as a second or other language
ESW	education social worker
EWO	education welfare officer
EY	early years
EYDCP	Early Years Development Childcare Partnerships www.surestart.gov.uk/

FAS	Funding Agency for Schools
FASNA	Foundation and Aided Schools National Association www.fasna.org.uk
FE	further education
FEFC	further education funding council
FEI	further education institution
FHE	Further and Higher Education
FOI	freedom of information
FS	feeder school
FSA	Food Standards Agency www.food.gov.uk/
FSM	free school meals
FTE	full-time equivalent
FTET	full-time education and training
GB	governing body
GPT	guaranteed planning time
GRTP	graduate and registered teacher programme
GT	gifted and talented
GTCE	General Teaching Council for England www.gtce.org.uk/
GTCS	General Teaching Council for Scotland www.gtcs.org.uk
GTCW	General Teaching Council for Wales www.gtcw.org.uk
GTP	graduate teacher programme
GTTR	Graduate Teacher Training Registry www.gttr.ac.uk/
HE	higher education
HEA	health education authority
HEI	higher education institution
HI	hearing impaired
HLTA	higher level teaching assistant
HMCI	Her Majesty's Chief Inspector of Schools
HMI	Her Majesty's inspectors
HoD	head of department
HoS	head of school
HoY	head of year
HSE	Health and Safety Executive www.hse.gov.uk/
HSI	Healthy Schools Initiative

HT	headteacher
IAP	individual action plan
IC	information commissioner www.informationcommissioner.gov.uk
ICG	Institute of Careers Guidance www.icg-uk.org/
ICT	information and communications technology
IEP	individual education plan
IiP	Investors in People www.investorsinpeople.co.uk
IiYP	Investors in Young People
ILP	information and learning technology
INSET	in-service education and training
IRT	identification referral and tracking
ISC	Independent Schools Council www.isc.co.uk/
ITE	initial teacher education
ITT	initial teacher training
IWB	interactive white board
JMI	junior, middle and infant
KS	key stage
LA	local authority
LD	level description
LEA	local education authority
LSA	learning support assistant
LSAC	Language, sports and arts college
LSC	Learning and Skills Council www.lsc.gov.uk
LSP	learning strategy partnership
LSU	learning support unit
MA	modern apprenticeships www.apprenticeships.org.uk/
MFL	modern foreign languages
MLD	moderate/mild learning difficulties
MNS	maintained nursery school
NAACE	National Association of Advisors for Computers in Education www.naace.org/
NACCCE	National Advisory Committee on Creative and Cultural Education
NACCEG	National Advisory Council for Careers and Educational Guidance

NACE	National Association for Able Children in Education www.nace.co.uk/
NACETT	National Advisory Council on Education and Training Targets
NAGC	National Association for Gifted Children www.nagc.org
NAS	National Autistic Society www.nas.org.uk
NASEN	National Association for Special Educational Needs www.nasen.org.uk/
NASUWT	National Association of Schoolmasters/Union of Women Teachers www.teachersunion.org.uk/
NATSOC	National Society for Promoting Religious Education www.natsoc.org.uk/
NC	National Curriculum www.ncaction.org.uk/
NCET	National Council for Educational Technology
NCPTA	National Confederation of Parent Teacher Associations www.ncpta.org.uk/
NCS	National Childcare Strategy
NCT	national curriculum test (see NT)
NEOST	National Employers' Organisation for School Teachers www.lg-employers.gov.uk
NFER	National Foundation for Educational Research www.nfer.ac.uk/index.cfm
NGfL	National Grid for Learning www.ngfl.gov.uk/
NHSS	National Healthy Schools Standard www.wiredforhealth.gov.uk/
NLS	National Literacy Strategy www.standards.dfes.gov.uk/literacy
NLT	National Literacy Trust www.literacytrust.org.uk
NNS	National Numeracy Strategy www.standards.dfes.gov.uk/numeracy
NOF	New Opportunities Fund www.nof.org.uk/
NoR	number on roll
NQT	newly qualified teacher
NT	national test (often referred to as SAT)
NUT	National Union of Teachers www.teachers.org.uk/
NVQ	National Vocational Qualification

OECD	Organisation for Economic Cooperation and Development www.oecd.org/
Ofsted	Office for Standards in Education www.ofsted.gov.uk/
OSHL	out of school hours learning
OTT	overseas trained teacher
PAFT	parents as first teachers
PANDA	performance and assessment data
PEP	personal education plan
PFI	private finance initiative
PI	performance indicators
PM	performance management
PMLD	profound and multiple learning difficulties
PNS	Primary National Strategy
PNW	pupil needs weighting
PoS	programme of study
PPA	planning, preparation and assessment
PPP	public private partnership
PROLOG	The DfES publishing department: 0845 6022260, dfes@prolog.uk.com
PRP	performance related pay
PRU	pupil referral unit
PSA	parent staff association
PSE	personal and social education
PSHE	personal, social and health education
PSLD	physical and severe learning difficulties
PSP	pastoral support programme
PT	part time
PTA	parent teacher association
PTR	pupil teacher ratio
QCA	Qualifications and Curriculum Authority www.qca.org.uk
QTS	qualified teacher status
REEF	Race Employment and Education Forum
RgI/RI	registered inspector
RPA	regional provider of assessment
SAC	Scottish Arts Council www.scottisharts.org.uk

SACRE	Standing Advisory Council on Religious Education
SAI	School Access Initiative
SCAA	School Assessment and Curriculum Authority
SCD	severe communication difficulties
SCITT	school centred initial teacher training
SDP	school development plan
SEN	special educational needs
SENCO	special educational needs coordinator
SEP	single education plan
SLD	severe learning difficulties
SLDD	students with learning difficulty and/or disability
SLT	senior leadership team
SMT	senior management team
SRE	sex and relationship education
SRS	safer routes to school
SSD	social services department
SSE	school self-evaluation
SVQ	Scottish Vocational Qualification
TA	teaching assistant
TC	technology college
TDA	Training and Development Agency for Schools www.tda.gov.uk/
TEC	Training and Enterprise Council
TESSS	The Extended Schools Support Service www.continyou.org.uk/
TUC	Trades Union Congress
UNESCO	United Nations Educational, Scientific and Cultural Organisation www.unesco.org
VA School	voluntary aided school
VC School	voluntary controlled school
VI	visually impaired
VLE	virtual learning environment
VTC	virtual teacher centre
WAMG	Workforce Agreement Monitoring Group

Index

Page numbers in italic show **Tables**